THE MAKING OF THE SOUTH YORKSHI

THE MAKING OF THE SOUTH YORKSHIRE LANDSCAPE

A popular guide to the history of the county's countryside and townscapes

Melvyn Jones

WITH LINE ILLUSTRATIONS BY BOB WARBURTON

Wharncliffe Books

First Published in 2000 by
Wharncliffe Books
an imprint of
Pen and Sword Books Limited,
47 Church Street, Barnsley,
South Yorkshire. S70 2AS

Copyright © Melvyn Jones and Bob Warburton 2000

For up-to-date information on other titles produced under the
Wharncliffe imprint, please telephone or write to:

Wharncliffe Books
FREEPOST
47 Church Street
Barnsley
South Yorkshire S70 2BR
Telephone (24 hours): 01226 - 734555

ISBN: 1-871647-75-4

A CIP catalogue record of this book is available from the
British Library

Cover illustrations:
Tankersley (top left); Tickhill (top right); Sheffield (bottom left); Gallery Bottom Wood, Rotherham (bottom right).
All photographs by the Author.

Printed in Great Britain by
Redwood Books, Trowbridge, Wiltshire

CONTENTS

ACKNOWLEDGEMENTS

I owe a great debt of gratitude to all those who, over the years, have knowingly and unknowingly fed and sustained my interest in the countryside and in landscape and industrial history: Frank Ellerby at the Holgate Grammar School, Barnsley; Professor Kenneth Edwards and Dr Joan Fuller at the University of Nottingham; the writings of Maurice Beresford, Michael Chisholm, E. Estyn Evans, David Hey, W. G. Hoskins, Emrys Jones, Richard Muir, Oliver Rackham, Carl Sauer and Christopher Taylor; colleagues Bill Hornby, Tom Randle and Ian Rotherham; and fellow writers on South Yorkshire's history, Arthur Clayton, Brian Elliott and Trevor Lodge. To all of them a big thank you. I also wish to thank Bob Warburton for agreeing to take on the task of translating my rough ideas for maps and diagrams into the finished products which adorn this book. Last, but most importantly, I wish to thank my wife Joan for sharing my interests, preparing the packed lunches, driving me round the countryside, taking photographs, and for reading and commenting on every chapter.

Melvyn Jones
Thorpe Hesley
December, 1999

Introduction: A Diverse and Many-Layered Landscape

THE PHYSICAL LANDSCAPE of South Yorkshire - the moorlands and valleys, the hills and vales, the plateaus and plains, and the soils that clothe them - has had an immense influence on the way in which human beings over thousands of years have created the **human landscape** - a landscape gradually filled with farms, hamlets, villages, towns, roads, canals and railways and all the other major and minor features that constitute the South Yorkshire landscape at the beginning of the twenty-first century.

Anyone who has travelled from west to east or east to west across the county will be fully aware of the great contrasts of altitude and relief (Figure 1.1). Let us take, for example, a journey by car from the moorlands in the south-west of the county to the west of Bradfield, to Thorne in the extreme north-east. In the extreme west, beyond Bradfield, are bleak uninhabited moorlands, at their highest approaching 548 metres above sea level, cut through by the headwaters of the Derwent, and the Don and its tributaries. The skyline is periodically dominated by westward facing edges. The altitude decreases eastwards and eventually at and beyond the valley of the Upper Don the country takes on a more rolling appearance and drops from about 244 metres. to less than 39 metres in the dozen miles (19 km) between Grenoside and Thurnscoe. Another distinct, but lower edge is then met with, rising to nearly 110 metres at Hickleton, beyond which is a low plateau of fertile agricultural country that gives way at Doncaster and beyond to a flat lowland at places no more than a few metres above sea level.

Figure 1.1. Contrasting South Yorkshire landscapes. A. Hill country to the west of Bradfield at over 1,000 metres. B. The River Idle, which in this section forms the eastern boundary of South Yorkshire with Nottinghamshire. The surrounding land is only five metres above sea level. The Author

A.

B.

GEOLOGY

These dramatic variations in relief and altitude reflect the underlying geology (Figure 1.2).

The solid geology of South Yorkshire is made up of a a series of **sedimentary rocks**, thousands of feet thick and laid down from 200 million to 300 million years ago. Sedimentary rocks are so called because they were originally sediments - animal and mineral - deposited in ancient seas, lagoons and deltas. They were then folded, uplifted, tilted and eroded to give us today's scenery.

In the west beyond the valleys of the Upper Don and the Sheaf the underlying geology is the so-called Millstone Grit

Series made up of shales and gritstones which originated as muds and coarse sands respectively deposited in vast deltas from rivers from a continent to the north. These shales and grits have been subject to uplift and tilting to the north-east so that those exposed in South Yorkshire are the eastern half of a great dome. Large parts of the Millstone Grit country are over 328 metres where featureless expanses of moorland are broken by rocky outcrops or edges.

To the east of the Millstone Grit country lie the Coal Measures. These are made up of sediments laid down in a changing coastal environment in which forests developed and then subsided beneath layers of mud and sand. This cycle of forest environment succeeded by deposition and subsidence was repeated over and over again giving rise to a characteristic sequence today of coal seam, shale, sandstone and seatearth. In the western half of the Coal Measure country the sandstones form a system of broken but bold edges the most significant being at Wharncliffe Crags which rise to 250 metres.

The closely grouped edges in the west give way to the east to broad vales and minor edges because of the more extensive shale deposits and thinner sandstones. A special feature of the Coal Measures is that in the western half coal seams outcrop at the surface and then dip eastwards getting progressively deeper until they disappear

Figure 1.2. *Geology of South Yorkshire.*

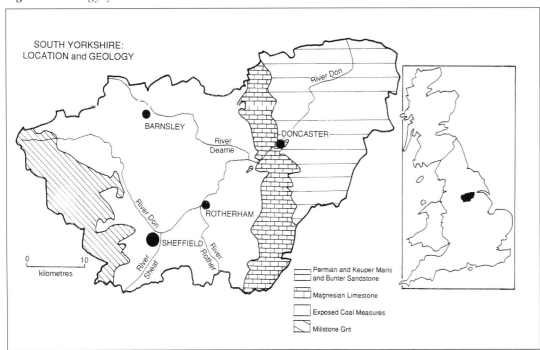

beneath the extra thicknesses of younger rocks to the east.

The eastern boundary of the Coal Measures is marked by an elevated strip of country, this time capped by limestone, which extends for a width of four or five miles from the northern to the southern boundary of the county. It overlooks the Coal Measures in the form of a low escarpment (edge) and contains another low escarpment running parallel to the first. The limestone, called Magnesian Limestone, is the result of the deposition of marine animals in shallow lagoons and coastal waters. The Magnesian Limestone country is gently rolling and a fertile red soil has developed which made the area the most attractive in the county for early settlement. At Sprotbrough the Don flows through a gap in the limestone escarpment, as does Maltby Dike at Roche Abbey, 10 km further south. At Conisbrough faulting has caused part of the limestone outcrop to be detached from the main escarpment thus providing the commanding site for Conisbrough and its castle.

Finally, marls (a mixture of clay and calcium carbonate) and sandstones, deposited in ancient salt lakes and deserts respectively, form the bedrocks of the extensive lowlands to the east of Doncaster, sometimes referred to as the Humberhead Levels. These lowlands were covered with gravels, clays and silts in the glacial and immediate post-glacial period and then flooded in late prehistoric times at a time of rising sea levels. In places there are deep layers of peat beneath mires and bogs; in others the marls and sandstones appear as low islands of slightly elevated land.

LANDSCAPE CHARACTER

Each of the four geological zones described above - the Millstone Grit country, the Coal Measures, the Magnesian Limestone escarpment, and the Humberhead Levels have a characteristic mixture of human landscape elements, shaped in various ways by the underlying geology, and the related topography, soils and climate and these form the basis for identifying what the Countryside Commission (now the Countryside Agency) have called landscape character areas. Five **landscape character areas** can be recognised in South Yorkshire as shown in Figures 1.3 and 1.4. Their key characteristics are summarised below.

Dark Peak

This area is composed of exposed, bleak plateaus with dramatic gritstone edges on the highest parts of the Millstone Grit country. Large stretches are covered with heather moorland and blanket bog, without a sign of habitation. Deep narrow valleys carrying fast-flowing river headwaters fringe the area, sometimes heavily wooded on the steep valley sides. The larger valleys contain reservoirs. At lower levels on the eastern margins are pastures enclosed by drystone walls.

Figure 1.3. *Landscape character areas.*

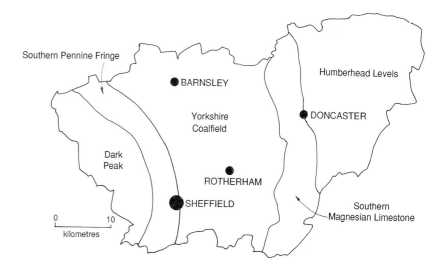

Figure 1.4. *Landscapes in the five landscape character areas of South Yorkshire. A. Uninhabited moorland and unimproved grazing land in the Dark Peak. B. Enclosed farmland in the Southern Pennine Fringe. C. Restoration of industrial land in the Coalfield area. D. Rolling farmland in the Magnesian Limestone belt. E. A riverside village (Fishlake) in the Humberhead Levels.* The Author

Settlement is largely dispersed with the gritstone buildings sitting low within the landscape.

Southern Pennine Fringe

This narrow zone embraces both the lower eastern fringes of the Millstone Grit country and the higher western parts of the Coal Measure country and includes the western half of the City of Sheffield. It is crossed by the steep sided valleys of the Upper Don and by its tributaries the Little Don, Loxley and Rivelin. These valleys have been industrialised in places and the industrial buildings and their accompanying ribbons of settlement and lines of transport contrast strongly with the ancient drystone-walled field systems and woodland on the surrounding hillsides. Settlement is a very varied mixture with villages such as the suburbanised Oughtibridge and Grenoside, the estate village of Wortley, the old market town of Penistone, the industrial town of Stocksbridge dominated by its steelworks, and the attractive western suburbs of Sheffield.

Yorkshire Coalfield

This area is characterised by its rolling landscape of low escarpments and broad valleys and vales occupied by a complex mosaic of large urban areas (the whole of Barnsley and Rotherham and the eastern half of Sheffield), untidy and sprawling, small, ex-mining towns sometimes forming urban ribbons, as between Worsbrough, Wombwell and Wath and between Rawmarsh, Swinton and Mexborough, estate villages such as Wentworth, neat 'rural' villages such as Cawthorne and suburbanised villages such as Silkstone and Thorpe Hesley. On the edges of and between many of these settlements, farming landscapes, with a mixture of hedged and walled fields, survive, as do many ancient woods. Well wooded parkland landscapes also survive intact as at Wortley, Wentworth Castle and Wentworth Woodhouse. The area is

criss-crossed by transport networks old and new: trunk roads, motorways, railways, supertram routes and canals. Derelict industrial and mining sites, often tumbling down to secondary woodland, dot the landscape. Larger tracts of restored and landscaped former industrial land, some now given over to recreational use, others to the sites of new industrial estates, edge of town shopping centres and distribution depots are major features of the landscape. Building materials are mixed: the older buildings are in local sandstone, but large areas of late nineteenth and twentieth century building are in brick and slate, with groups of post-industrial buildings in modern materials such as concrete, steel and glass.

Southern Magnesian Limestone

This area is in the form of a narrow ridge a few miles across from west to east. It is elevated and quite distinct from the coalfield character area to the west but to the east it merges imperceptibly with the lowlands forming the Humberhead Levels. In South Yorkshire this ridge is broken only at Sprotbrough and at Maltby. The traditional buildings in the area, including a number of important parish churches, the castles at Conisbrough and Tickhill and the abbey at Roche, are constructed of the creamy limestone often with pantile roofs. The main settlements are separated from each other by extensive tracts of rolling agricultural land dominated by arable crops in large fields with low hawthorn hedges. The area also contains well wooded estate landscapes as at Brodsworth and Sandbeck. The area is, however, not without its industrial features, containing mining villages at New Edlingon, Maltby and Dinnington.

Humberhead Levels

This extensive lowland was once occupied by a large glacial lake in which great thicknesses of silt and gravel were deposited covering the marls and sandstones below. This is, therefore, mainly a flat agricultural landscape improved over centuries by drainage schemes large and small and by warping (the inundation of the land in winter leading to the deposition of rich tidal silts). The flatness of the landscape is emphasised to the west of the Don by the use of dykes as field boundaries and the relatively small numbers of hedgerows and trees. Large peat bogs exist at Hatfield and Thorne, exploited for commercial peat production but also containing areas of outstanding ecological and archaeological importance. The oldest settlements are located on what in early times would have been small islands among the extensive fenland and along riverbanks formed by the protruding bedrock and deposits of sand and gravel as at Thorne, Sykehouse, Arksey, Bentley and Fishlake. More modern settlement is mostly in the form of isolated agricultural dwellings scattered across the lowlands. Intruding into this predominantly rural scene are a number of modern mining villages as at Stainforth, New Rossington and Armthorpe, although Rossington Colliery is one of only two remaining collieries in South Yorkshire. The eastern suburbs of Doncaster (of which Armthorpe is now a part) have also extended into the area. Finally a major feature of this landscape are the cooling towers of Thorpe Marsh power station which can be seen from long distances.

A MANY-LAYERED LANDSCAPE

Not only is the human landscape of South Yorkshire extremely varied, it also has great **depth**, having developed over thousands of years. Although many early features have been swept away or buried beneath modern developments, many have survived and are taken for granted as part of the modern scene. The present-day landscape, therefore, is made up of features from every age: iron-age encampments exist alongside Roman roads, Romano-British settlement sites and field systems, Norman castles, medieval abbeys and parish churches, medieval deer parks, Tudor barns and domestic buildings, seventeenth and eighteenth century country houses and their landscaped parks, late eighteenth and early nineteenth century canal systems, Victorian railway networks, planned twentieth century mining villages, motorway networks, edge of and out of town shopping centres, modern sports stadia and arenas, and so on. The South Yorkshire landscape is **many-layered**. And to understand it we need to be able to peel away the layers.

To illustrate this the diagrams on the next page (Figure 1.5 A-D) show three stages in the evolution of the human landscape in the Upper Don and Wharncliffe areas of South Yorkshire, part of the Southern Pennine Fringe landscape character area described above.

Diagram A shows the physical landscape seen from the south, developed on eastward dipping Millstone Grit and Coal Measure sandstones and shales with seams of pot clay, ganister and thin coals. Occupying the central zone is the valley of the River Don. To the east lies the Greno-Wharncliffe upland rising to over 300 metres, and bounded in the north by the impressive Wharncliffe Crags composed of the outcropping Wharncliffe Rock. To the west tributary streams have carved valleys forming intervening rounded spurs giving way to the Pennine uplands rising to nearly 400 metres.

Diagram B shows the area in the Iron Age / Romano-British Period (c. 700 BC - 400 AD) in which the area and its resources were intensively exploited. The oak-birch woods were cleared in the upland areas and occupied by settlements and field systems. No less than eighteen Romano-British sites have been located in the Greno-Wharncliffe upland.

Diagram C shows how the landscape had developed by the sixteenth century. Woodland clearance was much further advanced and the remaining woods, of which Wharncliffe,

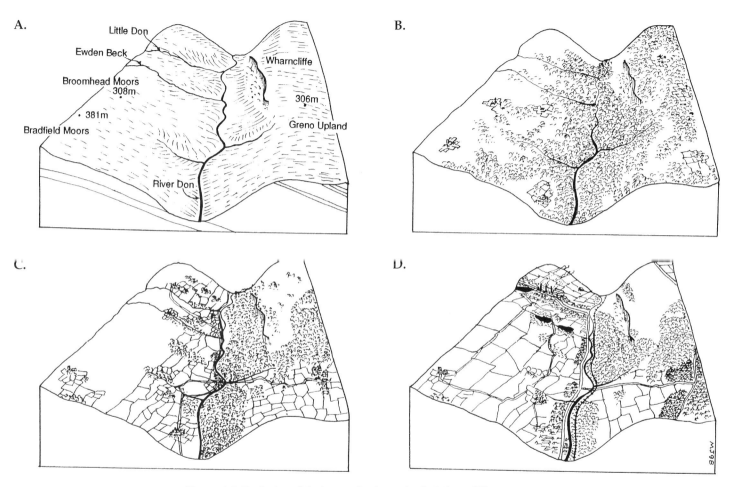

A.

Little Don

Ewden Beck

Wharncliffe

Broomhead Moors
308m

306m

• 381m

Greno Upland

Bradfield Moors

River Don

B.

C.

D.

Figure 1.5. *Evolution of the human landscape in the Wharncliffe-Upper Don area.*

Greno and Beeley were the largest, were either coppices or were enclosed within Wharncliffe Chase, a refuge for red deer, with a splendid lodge, belonging to the Wortley family.

Hamlets such as Grenoside, Oughtibridge and Deepcar, together with a large number of individual farms, were surrounded by small, irregularly shaped, hedged and walled fields resulting from clearance of woodland and connected to each other by a network of lanes and tracks. Unenclosed higher land to the west of the Don was exploited for peat and supported grazing animals. Water power sites were also an important feature of the landscape by this time.

Diagram D shows the modern landscape. Not surprisingly, many changes have taken place since the end of the sixteenth century. The Little Don valley has been industrialised and the industrial settlement of Stocksbridge created; urban requirements for water supplies have added reservoirs to the landscape; hamlets have become villages and have become suburbanised; large areas of surviving woodland have been coniferised; the open moorland has been enclosed; and the route of a once important trans-Pennine railway and modern roads cross the area. But a surprisingly large number of features from earlier periods have survived and the landscape is many-layered and rich in heritage.

The rest of this book is concerned with disentangling the complicated story of the development of the many-layered human landscape of South Yorkshire.

Map coverage

The county is covered by Ordnance Survey 1:50,000 sheets 110 (Sheffield and Huddersfield) and 111 (Sheffield and Doncaster). The 1:25000 O. S. Pathfinder series sheets are essential for detailed explorations. Also useful are Alan Godfrey's republished large scale O. S. maps of parts of South Yorkshire. They are usually maps of selected areas in *c.* 1900.

Aerial photographic cover

From January 2000 it is possible to view via the Internet vertical aerial coverage of the whole of England. To get a bird's eye view of anywhere in South Yorkshire simply visit www.millennium-map.com

Places to visit

The broad sweep of the South Yorkshire countryside can be viewed from a number of outstanding viewpoints:

Community Centre car park, Grenoside (grid reference SK332938) for views **eastwards** over the Coal Measures and Magnesian Limestone escarpment towards the Humberhead Levels.

Owler Bar (SK294780) for views from the moorland edge over Sheffield and the Coal Measures.

M1 driving north between exits 29 and 30, for views westwards towards the Pennines.

Western end of Church Corner (lane to south of church) at Laughton en le Morthen (SK516882) on the very edge of the Magnesian limestone escarpment looking westwards over the Coal Measures towards the Pennines.

Houghton Common (Great Houghton, SK431087) for views south-west over the coalfield in the direction of the Pennines.

HUNTER-GATHERERS AND THE FIRST FARMED LANDSCAPES

ALTHOUGH HUMAN BEINGS roamed, hunted and sought shelter over hundreds of thousands of years during warm periods between periods of glaciation in what we know today as South Yorkshire, the story of permanent settlement and the beginnings of the shaping of the modern landscape did not begin until several thousand years after the end of the last glaciation about 12,000-10,000 years ago.

HUNTER-GATHERERS OF THE OLD STONE AGE

The peoples who roamed the South Yorkshire landscapes in the inter-glacial periods before about 10,000 BC were hunter-gatherers. They were the Palaeolithic (Old Stone Age) peoples whose shelters were crudely constructed, or in caves, and whose tools and weapons were of stone (Figure 2.1(a)) or bone. They survived by hunting the 'big game' that lived in the area - animals such as bison, horse and red deer in the warmest periods of forest vegetation, and mammoth, woolly rhinoceros and reindeer when the climate deteriorated and tundra conditions prevailed with only moss, lichens, coarse grass, and low growing and stunted bushes to sustain the animal populations. In the severest climatic periods - which could last for tens of thousands of years - the ground was permanently below moving ice sheets and the human population left the area, only to move northwards into the area again when the ice sheets retreated. On present evidence, settlement may have been absent altogether for about 15,000 years before the end of the last glaciation. The human population would have been small at the best of times and each small group would have developed a cycle of movements over a well-known territory following the seasonal movements of the animals they hunted.

Ice movement and the associated scouring of the landscape have removed a great deal of archaeological evidence but Palaeolithic tools and weapons have survived in river gravels (the closest example to South Yorkshire being those in the Trent valley near Nottingham) and in caves, including Deadman's Cave in Anston Stones Wood on the Magnesian Limestone.

The most important Palaeolithic site in the north Midlands is just outside South Yorkshire at Creswell Crags in North Derbyshire. The valley cut by a stream there through the Magnesian Limestone, formed a natural migration route for animals and the cliffs on either side of the valley contained

Figure 2.1. (a) Palaeolithic flint tools from Pin Hole Cave, Creswell, (b) bone decorated with reindeer, Pin Hole Cave, Creswell; (c) Mesolithic microliths, Deepcar; (d) Neolithic polished stone axe, Wharncliffe; (e) Bronze spearhead, Stannington; (f) Bronze axe, Wybourn estate; (g) Bronze palstave, Rivelin valley, Sheffield.

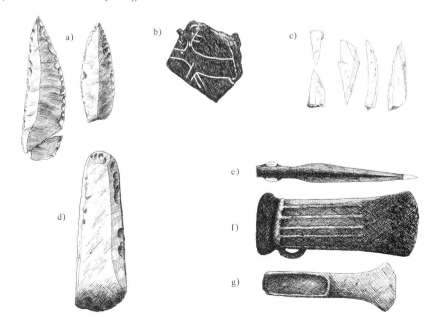

natural caves. In the late Palaeolithic, during and immediately following the retreat of the ice sheets and the beginnings of climatic and vegetational change, the area must have formed a natural hunting ground flanked by natural shelters. The deposits on the floors of the caves have not only yielded the bones of animals such as mammoth, woolly rhinoceros, hyena, arctic fox, horse, elk and reindeer, but also a wide selection of stone tools of flint and quartzite (from local pebbles) such as leaf-shaped spearheads, scrapers (used in preparing animal skins) and bone needles and burins (engraving tools for cutting bone and splintering antlers). Pieces of engraved bone have also been discovered (Figure 2.1(b).

HUNTER-GATHERERS OF THE POST – GLACIAL FORESTS

Rising temperatures 12,000 years ago resulted in the melting and shrinking of the most recent glaciers and ice sheets which led to a rise in sea levels around neighbouring coasts and, by about 6,000 BC, the creation of Great Britain as an island separated from the continent, rather than a westward extension of mainland Europe. The rising temperatures also resulted in the thawing of frozen ground and, most importantly, in a gradual change in vegetation culminating, by about 7,000 BC, in the development of a more or less continuous tree cover - the primaeval woods that have become known as the 'wildwood'.

Seeds borne on the wind or spread in the droppings of birds and mammals enabled a wave of tree colonisation to make its way across the British Isles from the south-east. The progress of the colonisation has been reconstructed by using the pollen grains produced by trees, which are very resistant to decay, and which accumulated in bogs, lakes and ponds. Microscopic analysis enables the pollen of one species of tree to be distinguished from that of another. Using this evidence, it has been possible to show that the first trees to colonise post-glacial Britain were arctic trees such as aspen, birch and willow, the last two of which are still usually the first trees to grow on bare ground. Later came pine and hazel, then alder and oak. Later still came elm and lime and finally ash, holly, hornbeam and maple. The later trees found it more difficult to spread because the bare ground had already been occupied by the early colonisers. There then followed a long period of adjustment as particular species consolidated their dominance in particular localities, failed to gain a foothold in others or were pushed out by other invasive species. Between 8,000-5,000 BC the wildwood, a term coined by the Cambridge ecologist, Oliver Rackham, to describe Britain's woods before they were interfered with by humans, became fully developed.

No one knows what the wildwood looked like. There must have been many very old, very large trees and, where these had crashed down, thickets of young growth. There must also

Figure 2.2. The wildwood.

have been many dead trees: standing, leaning against neighbours and lying on the woodland floor in various stages of decomposition. Pollen analysis suggests that there were permanent glades of varying sizes scattered throughout the wildwood which would have been grazed and kept treeless by wild cattle, wild pig and deer (Figure 2.2).

As the environment changed from tundra to forest after 10,000 BC the surviving human population gradually began to subsist on smaller prey (mammals, fish and birds) of forest, marsh, river and lake and the more abundant fruits, nuts and roots. Mammals included wild cattle, red deer, wild pig, horse, bear and beaver. The bow and arrow had been invented by this time, a weapon particularly well suited for silent and patient hunting in a wooded environment. These forest hunter-fisher-gatherers are known as the Mesolithic (Middle Stone Age) peoples. For most of their occupation of what is now South Yorkshire, their impact on the natural landscape, like that of their Palaeolithic predecessors would have been negligible. Virtually all they left behind in South Yorkshire were their tools and their weapons, although seasonal camps built on timber platforms at the water's edge which have been found in the Vale of Pickering and the Somerset Levels, may still await discovery in the Humberhead Levels beyond Doncaster. The largest numbers of finds have occurred on the moorlands in the western parts of the county where they have been preserved beneath peat deposits and then revealed as the peat has eroded. Finds have been rarer on the central Coal Measures due to early and continuous disturbance by later cultures and burying under residential and industrial developments, but important finds of artefacts have been made at Deepcar, Wincobank, Hooton Roberts and Canklow. At Deepcar, for example, what appears to have been a temporary camp beside the River Don, where flint tools had been prepared, yielded more than 23,000 artefacts (including debris from working flints). There were signs of a shelter, possibly a windbreak, around three hearths.

The most characteristic artefact of the late Mesolithic period is the microlith, i.e. a very small worked stone, most commonly flint or chert (flintlike quartz). A microlith is either in the shape of a very small arrowhead or a barb, and these would have been fitted into a wooden shaft to make a multi-faceted arrow, harpoon or spear suitable for hunting the prey found in the forests, lakes and rivers of South Yorkshire (Figure 2.1 (c)).

In the late Mesolithic period hunting became more intensive and the forest environment appears to have been managed in places by felling and burning the wildwood to entice deer into areas of new, highly palatable, growth. This development foreshadowed the later domestication of pigs, sheep and cattle.

THE FIRST FARMERS

While the Mesolithic peoples of South Yorkshire were following their hunting-fishing-gathering lifestyle, a 'revolution' was taking place in the Middle East and Mediterranean Europe. This was the development of agriculture from about 8,000 BC, accompanied by pottery making and weaving. This agricultural revolution involved the domestication of pigs, sheep, cattle, the breeding of horses, the invention of ploughing, the systematic growing of cereals and, of course, an eventual change from a semi-nomadic existence to one where sites were occupied on a more or less permanent basis.

These innovations spread to Europe through the colonisation of new lands by farmers and by adoption by hunter-gatherers through contact with farmers, reaching the British Isles between 3,000-4,000 BC. There is much debate among archaeologists about the relative importance of colonisation from mainland Europe as opposed to the native hunter-gatherer population simply changing from one way of surviving to another. Colonists must have introduced sheep and cereals because these are not native to Britain.

At first, settled pioneering farming communities would have co-existed side by side with hunter-gatherer groups but by about 3000 BC farming, predominantly animal rearing, had replaced hunter-gathering as the main means of subsistence in what is now South Yorkshire. This is what has traditionally been referred to as the Neolithic (New Stone) Age.

Despite the great significance of the change from hunting and gathering to breeding and rearing domesticated animals and eventually to mixed farming, tools were still of stone. But they were 'finished' more expertly, e.g., polished axes of various igneous rocks from other regions which must have been acquired by trade. In addition, new tools appeared, e.g., flint sickles for harvesting wheat and barley. Unlike the neighbouring county of Derbyshire, no Neolithic settlements or sacred monuments have been found in South Yorkshire, and so the presence of a Neolithic population in the county is known largely from chance finds of stone tools (Figure 2.1 (d)). However, two Neolithic burial mounds (barrows) have been found on the Magnesian Limestone plateau at Dinnington and Sprotborough. The one at Dinnington was opened and destroyed in 1862, when it was reported that it contained fifteen burials.

A series of later cultures succeeded the Neolithic in the rest of the prehistoric period and in the succeeding period of Roman rule (the term Romano-British is used to describe native British settlements in this period). In each case there was a time lag between these new cultures arriving in Britain and evidence of their penetration into South Yorkshire. The Bronze Age in South Yorkshire and surrounding counties, which succeeded the Neolithic, probably began about 1650 BC. Although stone continued to be used for tool and weapon

manufacture, this culture marked the beginning of the use of smelted metals. Bronze is an alloy produced by smelting copper with tin. Bronze tools and ornaments from this period include daggers, axes, spearheads and decorative pins (Figure 2.1 (e), (f) and (g)). They have been recovered from round burial barrows on the Millstone Grit moors and as chance finds. Other surviving features of the early Bronze Age on the moorlands in the west of the county are stone circles associated with burial customs, for example on Broomhead and Totley Moors, cairnfields (areas covered by piles of stone (cairns)) which may be associated with both clearance of land for agriculture and with burial, and rocks with cup-shape hollows and incised circles called cup and ring markings.

The Bronze Age was succeeded by the Iron Age in South Yorkshire about 700 BC. As its name implies, smelted iron tools succeeded those of bronze but this is likely to have been a slow process in South Yorkshire, distant from the main centres of technological change in the south of England. In South Yorkshire and neighbouring parts of West Yorkshire and Derbyshire, Iron Age burials are almost unknown but there are sixteen surviving forts, whose ramparts enclose areas ranging from 0.20 to 6.5 hectares. These were associated with surrounding farming communities and functioned as regional centres of military power and places of security for humans and animals in times of inter-tribal unrest.

An archaeological technique called radiocarbon dating enables the age of animal or vegetable remains (e.g., bone or charcoal) found at archaeological sites to be determined with a fair degree of accuracy. The technique, which uses sophisticated and sensitive equipment, is based on the fact that every organism has a fixed amount of radioactive isotope Carbon 14 present while it is living. At death Carbon 14 decays very slowly at a fixed rate. By measuring the amount of Carbon 14 in an archaeological sample it is possible to say how much time has elapsed since it died. The rampart timbers of the hill fort at Almondbury, near Huddersfield in West Yorkshire give a radiocarbon date in the sixth century BC, and charcoal from burnt rampart timber at the Wincobank fort gives a date of about 500 BC. The Iron Age forts of South Yorkshire are dealt with at greater length in Chapter 7.

Besides the forts, minor earthwork enclosures and field systems of the Iron Age and succeeding Romano-British period are features of hilltop and plateau locations in the lower parts of the Millstone Grit country and on the neighbouring Coal Measures. The best known examples are the Iron Age field systems in Canklow Wood and the numerous Romano-British sites on the escarpment between Wharncliffe and Grenoside.

Despite periods of unrest before, during and at the end of the Roman period (AD 43-410), local populations in the Neolithic, Bronze Age, Iron Age and Roman periods would have been largely engaged in farming activities. In this they were very successful. Slow population growth would have taken place, settlement

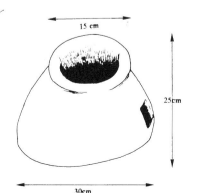

Figure 2.3. Beehive quern.

15 cm

25cm

30cm

would have spread and there would have been a considerable impact on the wildwood, as new sites were occupied for cereal growing and abandoned agricultural plots developed as very open woodland because of grazing pressure. Occupation of the Millstone Grit uplands during the Neolithic and Bronze ages led to widespread woodland clearance which, in periods of colder and wetter climate in the Iron Age and Roman periods, gave rise to the peat covered moorlands that we know today.

The intensity of cereal growing can be gauged from the fact that it gave rise in the Iron Age and Roman period to a quern making industry in the Loxley and Rivelin valleys and at Wharncliffe. Querns were hand operated grindstones for converting cereal grains into flour. The site at Wharncliffe is at the foot of the Crags (an outcrop of Wharncliffe Sandstone) and covers 72 hectares. On-site evidence of querns of different types and sizes suggests that the 'factory' may have had its origins in the Bronze Age and that it was still active in the medieval period, with its main phases of production in the Iron Age and Romano-British period. Thousands of 'flat-disc' and 'beehive' querns (see Figure 2.3) in various stages of production survive on the site. The name Wharncliffe is simply a corruption of Quern-cliff.

The almost county-wide occupation of the land by farmers during the Iron Age/Romano-British periods has been demonstrated most dramatically by Derrick Riley using aerial photography. Riley recorded crop marks in fields in South Yorkshire for more than two decades from 1970. Crop marks are of two kinds. Where ditches have been filled in, the soil is deeper and the crop grows better producing a deeper colour than elsewhere. Where there are buried wall foundations, crop roots are obstructed, the crop grows less well, and shows up in a lighter colour. Crop marks show up best when there are dry springs and hot summers. Derrick Riley's photographs have established the existence of networks of fields covering not only the Magnesian Limestone belt - which would have been expected to be densely settled by early farmers because of its light soils and gently rolling topography - but also on the Bunter sandstones further east and the Coal Measures to the west. Most of the crop marks were the result of the filling of enclosure ditches. The fields were of a regular rectangular shape, giving rise to a 'brickwork pattern' as shown in Figure 2.4.

Finally, it must not be thought that as our prehistoric ancestors changed from a hunter-gathering to a farming economy, involving the clearance of large tracts of the wildwood, that they lost contact with the post-glacial forest environment that they were transforming. They still hunted deer and wild boar, and wildfowl and fish, and they used timber and underwood for a myriad of purposes. They probably managed their surrounding woodlands and had to trade for wood if they no longer lived within a wooded environment. Nowhere has this continuing relationship

Figure 2.4. Crop marks showing a brickwork pattern near Edenthorpe, Doncaster. Based on aerial photographs by D. Riley, courtesy South Yorkshire Archaeological Service

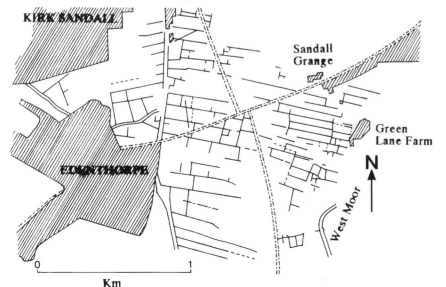

between prehistoric man and woods been more dramatically demonstrated than when the body of a Neolithic shepherd was found in a glacier in the Alps in 1991. His equipment included material from about a dozen different species of tree or shrub. His bow was of yew as was the haft of his copper axe; his arrow shafts were made from straight shoots of the wayfaring tree; his rucksack had a hazel and larch frame; he carried two containers made of birch bark, in one of which were kept his live embers for making a fire (charcoal made from elm and willow), wrapped in Norway maple leaves; his flint dagger had an ash handle; his retoucheur (for sharpening flint tools) consisted of a short section of a branch of a lime tree in which a splintered piece of stag's antler had been inserted. He carried cord made from bast - the inner bark of the lime tree. He even carried a piece of 'tinder' fungus (for lighting fires) and some birch bracket fungus which is believed was part of his travelling medicine kit.

What to read about the prehistoric period

BARNATT, J and SMITH, K. (1997) *Peak District,* Batsford / English Heritage.
DARVILL, T. (1987) *Prehistoric Britain,* Routledge.
RILEY, D. N. (1980) *Early Landscapes from the Air,* University of Sheffield.

Places to visit

Creswell Crags. Besides the valley and its caves there is a visitor centre with an interpretive display.

Weston Park Museum, Sheffield.
Extensive displays of prehistoric tools including Mesolithic microliths and other flint implements from Deepcar, and querns from Wharncliffe.

Doncaster Museum
Displays and artefacts from the Roman period.

PLACE-NAMES IN THE LANDSCAPE

OF ALL THE ELEMENTS in the landscape that give us a sense of identity, place-names are the most enduring (Figure 3.1). Names of hills, rivers, farms, hamlets, villages and towns, and routeways between and within settlements have stood the test of time through constant use. What must be remembered is that our ancestors did not have

Figure 3.1. Signpost to the past. Signpost at the crossroads in Chapeltown in the 1950s. There was a medieval chapel of ease at Chapeltown first recorded in Latin as Capella in 1260. Wortley was first recorded in the Domesday Book in 1086 as Wirtleie (clearing used for growing vegetables). Penistone was also first recorded in the Domesday Book and probably means hill farm (from the Celtic word for hill (penno) and Old English -tun). Wadsley Bridge was not recorded until 1427. Chapeltown & High Green Archive

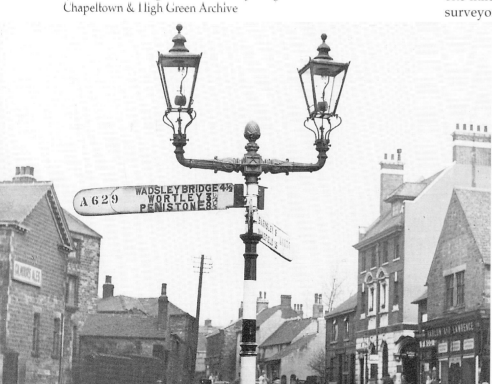

maps and there were few signposts - indeed most people would not have been able to read them if they had existed. What our ancestors did have were maps inside their heads - 'mental maps' - full of information passed down to them by their parents, grandparents and neighbours and augmented by their own experiences as their lives proceeded. This verbal passing on of the place-name geography of this country was punctuated by two great surveys that resulted in the systematic preservation of place-names: William the Conqueror's Domesday Survey of 1086 and the mapping of the country by the Ordnance Survey at a scale of one inch to one mile between about 1800 and 1850. But in both cases the surveyors relied on local people to give them accurate information.

Before proceeding further, it is worth noting one technical point. English place-names are either **simplex,** i.e., consisting of one element as in Marr or Wath, or **complex,** i.e., consisting of two or more elements such as in Shef/field or Barns/ley or Ross/ing/ton. Where there are two elements the first one is called the **prefix** and the second one the **suffix.**

THE CHRONOLOGY OF ENGLISH PLACE-NAMES

In a country which has seen a succession of invaders and colonists since Neolithic times, the place-names of any county will obviously be composed of a mixture of languages. In South Yorkshire six languages are represented in place-names (Figure 3.2):

(a) Celtic (or British) This is an ancestor of modern Welsh. It was spoken throughout England in the centuries before the Roman invasion of 43 AD, by the common people throughout the Roman occupation until about 410 AD, and in isolated places for some centuries afterwards. After the Anglo-Saxon invasions the language became increasingly restricted to the western fringes of Britain in Cumbria, Cornwall and Wales.

Figure 3.2. The chronology of English place-names.

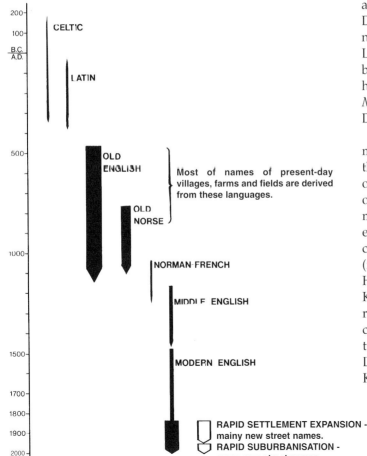

However, the Anglo-Saxons adopted Celtic names, especially those for natural features such as hills and rivers. Among Celtic names for natural features surviving in South Yorkshire are the river names Dearne, Dove and Rother, *penno* (hill) as in Penistone and *Rhos* (moor) as in Rossington. Another Celtic word is *egles* (meaning church) as in Ecclesall and Ecclesfield. *Don* as in River Don, may be pre-Celtic in origin; its meaning is unknown.

(b) Latin This language was used in Britain for administrative purposes during the Roman occupation. During this period it was the only written language. In the name Doncaster, the Anglo-Saxon *-ceaster* is derived from the Latin *castra,* a military fort. In the Middle Ages Latin again became the language of legal and administrative records and had some influence on place-names, e.g. the substitution of *Magna* for Great and *Parva* for Small. To the east of Rotherham Dalton Magna and Dalton Parva survive.

(c) Old English (Anglo-Saxon) This language, of which modern English is a much modified descendant, was used by the Anglo Saxons who settled the land and created thousands of villages, hamlets and farms from the mid-fifth century onwards. Old English evolved through Middle English to the modern English language. Most Old English names were in existence by Domesday. They tell of a farming people (the most common Old English suffixes in South Yorkshire are *-ham* (farm) as in Rotherham, *-tun* (farm) as in Darton, Treeton and Hickleton, and *-worth* (enclosure) as in Cudworth, Kimberworth and Wadworth. A woodland environment is reflected in place-name elements such as *-ley* (woodland clearing) as in Walkley, Barnsley and Cantley, *-field* (treeless tract in an otherwise wooded environment) as in Sheffield, Darfield and Austerfield and *-hurst* (wooded hill) as in Kilnhurst and Hazelhirst.

(d) Old Norse This was the language spoken by the Danish invaders who settled eastern England north of the Thames between the late ninth and late tenth centuries, and the Norwegian (Norse) settlers of northern England (who came from the west via Ireland). Together these two groups are known as the Vikings. South Yorkshire is particularly rich in Old Norse names (see below).

(e) Norman-French This was the language of William the Conqueror and his followers who invaded England in 1066. Their descendants eventually adopted the English language. Norman -French names are relatively rare. Two pure Norman-French names in South Yorkshire were formerly the names of abbeys: Beauchief which means 'beautiful headland' and Roche which means 'rock' and most probably refers to one of the rocky outcrops along the valley of Maltby Dike where the abbey of that name was founded in 1147; however, it could be a French translation of Stone, the name of a small settlement further down the valley from the abbey. Norman-French sometimes appears in place-names as an addition to earlier names, the extra name (called an **affix**) being a Norman-French family name as in Hooton Pagnell and Thorpe Salvin.

(f) Modern English There are surprisingly few modern settlement names - what may appear to be a new name is in many cases the re-working of an old name such as in the pit villages of Denaby Main, New Edlington and New Rossington, etc. Edenthorpe, the name of a Doncaster suburb, is a modern name and replaced the earlier Streetthorpe, the name of a settlement that appeared in Domesday Book but which had disappeared by the nineteenth century. Conanby, the Old Norse sounding name of a modern estate at Conisbrough is also a modern concoction.

THE VIKING HERITAGE IN SOUTH YORKSHIRE

The Vikings, as has already been pointed out, were Danes and Norwegians. In the ninth and tenth centuries they were short

of land as populations grew rapidly. They had also perfected the arts of boatbuilding and navigation at sea. They therefore had a reason for emigrating and a means of accomplishing it. The **Danes** started raiding the English coast in 793 AD when the monasteries of Jarrow and Lindisfarne were sacked and plundered. By about 850 they had begun wintering in the eastern counties and by 875 they were settling permanently in Yorkshire. First came tribal armies followed by farmers. Meanwhile **Norwegian** settlers were heading north and west to the coasts and islands of north-west Scotland and beyond to Ireland, Iceland, Greenland and North America. Eventually north-west England was settled by Norwegians from Ireland and the Isle of Man, Norwegian settlement later spreading to the south Pennines and its fringes. The Danes and Norwegians were collectively known as Vikings or Northmen (Norsemen). They spoke dialects of a language known as Old Norse.

South Yorkshire became a prime target for the Danes because it was accessible. The Danes came up the Humber and entered the area through the lower reaches of the Don and Trent and then up the valleys of the Dearne, Don and Rother. Danish ways eventually dominated East Anglia, the East Midlands and Yorkshire and this was formalised soon after 886 when a treaty between King Alfred, Saxon king of Wessex, and the Danes recognised the Danish dominated territory to the north and east of Watling Street which ran from London to Chester. This was called Danelaw. Here Danish populations were greatest, and their institutions and language had the greatest impact.

The former presence of the Danes in South Yorkshire is still felt in six ways:

Place-names in the landscape. The Danes in South Yorkshire established new settlements, took over existing settlements and changed the names of other settlements. A close study of the modern 1:50,000 Ordnance Survey sheets

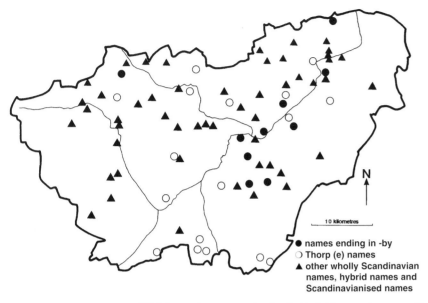

Street names in towns. The Old Norse word for a road, street or lane was *gata* which became gate. Barnsley has its Eastgate and Westgate (and Church Street used to be Kirkgate); Rotherham has Bridgegate, Doncaster Gate, Moorgate, Wellgate and several others now lost; Sheffield has Fargate and Waingate; Doncaster has Baxter Gate, High and Low Fisher Gate, French Gate, Friar's Gate, Hall Gate, St George Gate, and St Sepulchre Gate, and Tickhill has Westgate, Castlegate and Northgate. Such names are also found in small villages such as Westgate in Monk Bretton. The name was imported into the mining industry at an early date and anyone connected with coal mining will remember that the main roadway in a pit in South Yorkshire is called the main gate. The gate element is also found in the names of country lanes in South Yorkshire.

Ancient administrative systems (Figure 3.4). South Yorkshire was until 1974 part of the **West Riding** one of the three divisions of Yorkshire. Riding is a Danish word meaning a third. The Lindsey district of Lincolnshire was also divided

Figure 3.3. Old Norse place-names in South Yorkshire as shown on the Ordnance Survey 1:50,000 sheets 110 (Sheffield and Huddersfield) and 111 (Sheffield and Doncaster).

Figure 3.4. Viking administrative divisions in South Yorkshire.

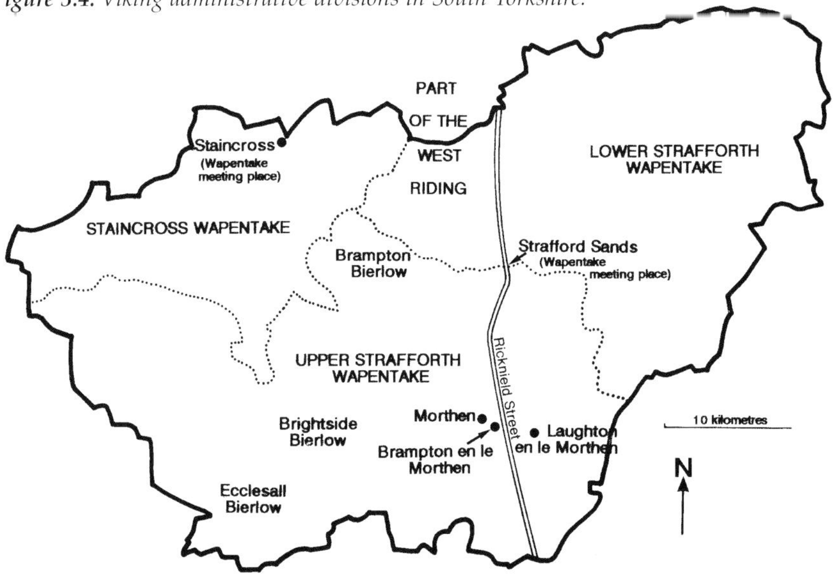

covering South Yorkshire (sheets 110 and 111) reveals more than 70 settlement names that are wholly or partly Viking in origin (Figure 3.3). The most common are those including the elements *-by* (farm, hamlet, village), *-thorpe* (daughter settlement) and *-thwaite* (woodland clearing). Many names are what are called hybrids, including both Old English and Old Norse elements, for example Wickersley (*Vikar's* [Old Norse personal name] woodland clearing [Anglo-Saxon *-ley*]) or Thurlestone (Thurulf's [Old Norse personal name] farm [Old English *-tun*]). Other Old English names were Scandinavianised, for example the *ch* sound was substituted with the *k* sound and the *sh* sound became *sk* so that the Old English Shelbrooke became Skelbrooke and Ashern became Askern.

into ridings. At a more local level South Yorkshire was divided into administrative divisions made up of groups of parishes, called **wapentakes.** In Anglo-Saxon counties these were called hundreds. Wapentake originally meant a gathering at which agreement was shown by brandishing weapons. More locally still, one group of settlements east of Rotherham had a local administrative assembly called by the Old Norse word *thing* (assembly). It took place in the countryside on a piece of moorland (uncultivated land) and was called the 'moor-thing'. This is perpetuated in the names Morthen, Brampton en le Morthen and Laughton en le Morthen. A document of 1345 recorded a meadow called *Tourneberg* on the lane between Upper Whiston and Morthen. *Tourneberg* means hill *(berg)* where a court *(tourn)* was held. Finally there are three communities, Brampton, Brightside and Ecclesall which until recently had the additional term 'Bierlow' attached to their names. This means village *(-by)* law. The modern term by-law (local law) is derived from this term. The name Brampton Bierlow is still shown on the modern Ordnance Survey map indicating a district rather than just the village of Brampton.

Words in standard English. There are at least a thousand words in modern English that have certainly been borrowed from Old Norse - e.g., awkward, birth, drown, crawl, fellow, happy, husband, leg, loose, odd, scare, skull, trust. In some cases we use Old English and Old Norse words interchangeably: we can rear (OE) or raise (ON) a child; we may wish (OE) for or want (ON) a beer; we can practise a craft (OE) or a skill (ON); and we can cure a hide (OE) or a skin (ON).

South Yorkshire dialect words. There are many thousands of dialect words of Old Norse origin used in those parts of England (and the lowlands of Scotland) once populated by Norwegians and Danes. Those used in South Yorkshire include: addle (to earn); band (string); dee (to die); ding (to hit as in a right old ding dong!); flag (as in flagstone); flit (move away); gawp (to stare); laik (to play); lig (to lie); loppy (dirty, verminous); muck (dirt, manure); reckon (think, consider), skitters (diarrhoea); skrike (shriek); stoup (post, gatepost).

Surnames. Many people in South Yorkshire carry Old Norse surnames: either after a place which was given an Old Norse name (e.g., Maltby, Micklethwaite, Osgathorpe, Scholes); or in the form of an Old Norse personal name (Thurston, Swain, Grimes) or from a former nickname (e.g., Tait (cheerful), Crook (crooked); and Coe (Jackdaw) or from an occupation (e.g., Skinner).

Many South Yorkshire people must carry Viking genes. Only DNA fingerprinting would show this. However, any reader whose family has lived locally for generations and has an Old Norse surname or two in their family tree could have Vikings as ancestors. A recent study has shown, for example, that long term residents of the central Lake District have the same DNA as people living in rural communities in South-west Norway! The Lake District was heavily settled by Norwegians in the tenth century.

A PLACE-NAME JOURNEY THROUGH SOUTH YORKSHIRE
It is impossible to deal with the meaning of every South Yorkshire place-name. What is attempted here is a 'virtual' journey through the county calling in at a number of particularly interesting and significant places and discussing the place-name origin.

The journey begins in Dore on the extreme south-west boundary of the county (Figure 3.5).

Dore was formerly in Derbyshire. The name is Old English and means literally what it says: a door, or in this case a place on a frontier giving access from one place to another: from the Anglo-Saxon kingdom of Mercia to the south to the Anglo-

Saxon kingdom of Northumbria to the north. It was here, on the boundary of the two kingdoms, that the Northumbrians submitted in 830 to Egbert of Wessex in order to avoid a military invasion.

Meersbrook originally referred to the stream of that name separating Sheffield parish from Norton parish. Meer means boundary. This small stream was also the boundary between Yorkshire and Derbyshire, between the Anglo-Saxon kingdoms of Northumbria and Mercia, and between the sees of the Archbishop of York and the Archbishop of Canterbury.

Storrs, first recorded in 1285, is a corruption of the Danish word *storth* meaning a wood. There are many names in the western half of South Yorkshire indicating a heavily wooded landscape in the past.

Ecclesfield means 'open country' (*-feld*) with a Celtic church (*egles*). The Anglo-Saxons who named the place borrowed the Celtic word for church. It is now generally believed that Ecclesfield was the ecclesiastical centre for a large Celtic estate that included the modern city of Sheffield and by the Middle Ages was known as Hallamshire.

Bradfield, first recorded in 1188, means a wide stretch (brad = broad) of treeless countryside (-field) in a predominantly wooded landscape. Other places in Bradfield parish indicating woodland or settlements in woodland clearings, besides Storrs (see above) include, Agden (oak valley), Brightholmlee (woodland clearing near the bright water meadow), Loxley (Locc's clearing), Whithamley (clearing among willows), and Ewden (yew valley).

Grenoside is a village on the hillside below *Gravenhou*, as it was first recorded in 1279. Gravenhou became Greno. The two elements in Gravenhou are *grafan* (excavation or quarry) and *haugr* or *hoh* (eminence or hill). So Grenoside means hillside or slope below the quarried hill. The

Grenoside Sandstone has long been quarried (Hillsborough Barracks (now Morrison's Superstore) and the Post Office in Fitzalan Square are both of Grenoside Sandstone).

Woodseats is one of a number of names (e.g. Norton Woodseats, Woodsetts, Wentworth Woodhouse) indicating colonisation of woodland, in the case of Norton Woodseats and Wentworth Woodhouse as daughter settlements of existing villages or hamlets. They are probably medieval in origin. Woodseats is still only a hamlet, divided into two by the A61, and right at the edge of Greno Wood.

Bromley, Wortley and Tankersley can be looked at together. The significant element in these names is *-ley* meaning a wood or a woodland clearing, again reflecting the once well-wooded landscape in which these names were given, probably in the seventh or eighth centuries.

Woolley is across the boundary in West Yorkshire but I cannot resist including it. It is another *-ley* name but the interesting element is the first part meaning wolves, so this was a clearing frequented by wolves. There are two mid-thirteenth century

Figure 3.5. A place-name journey through South Yorkshire.

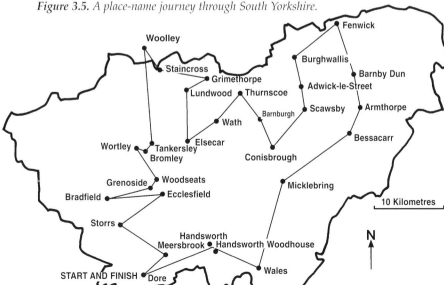

records of wolf pits being dug to trap wolves below Woolley Edge (e.g., *Wilfpit. . . super Colles de Wlvelei*). The last record of wolves in England was in the North York Moors in 1394-96. There is also Woolley in Ecclesfield and Woolthwaite between Maltby and Tickhill.

Staincross was the name of one of the ancient administrative sub-divisions of South Yorkshire (the others are Upper Strafforth and Lower Strafforth). The name means stone cross and is taken to mean the cross that stood at the Wapentake meeting place.

Grimethorpe and Lundwood. The first until recently a mining village and the other mainly a suburban council estate are both of ancient origin and have Old Norse (Danish) names. Grimethorpe means Grim's hamlet and lund in Lundwood is from *lundr* meaning a sacred grove of trees. Monk Bretton Priory whose ruins still stand at Lundwood was originally called St Mary Magdalene de Lunda.

Elsecar is an Old Norse name meaning Elsi's car (a carr is a marsh (Old Norse, *kjarr*)).

Wath is also an Old Norse name and means a ford across a river, in this case across the River Dearne.

Thurnscoe is also Old Norse and describes the vegetation of the area: Thorny (*thyrne*) wood (*skogr*).

Barnburgh is one of a substantial number of places in South Yorkshire with the Old English element burgh, borough or brough meaning a fortified place. Other such places include Masbrough, Conisbrough (still with its castle), Mexborough, Worsbrough, Stainborough and Kexbrough. Most of these fortifications were probably of pre-Saxon origin, and then re-named by the Saxon occupiers.

Conisbrough means the king's stronghold. The first part of the name is from the Old Norse *konungr* (king) but may have replaced the Anglo-Saxon *cyning* (king).

Scawsby is one of a growing number of places that are met as

one travels eastwards across the county with the *-by* element in its name, which is Old Norse meaning farm, hamlet or village. It is the commonest village name in Danelaw in which Danish and Norwegian peoples settled in the ninth and tenth centuries. Other South Yorkshire examples are Balby, Cadeby, Denaby (village of the Danes) and Maltby.

Adwick-le-Street is doubly interesting. The *-wick* is Anglo-Saxon for an isolated farm or dairy farm away from a village (= Adda's dairy farm). The Street element, which was first recorded in the mid-sixteenth century, refers to its location on the old Roman road, Ricknield Street, and distinguishes it from Adwick upon Dearne.

Burghwallis is another example of a burgh name (fortified site) with the addition of the family name of the lords of the manor in the thirteenth century.

Fenwick lies about 18 feet above sea level and originated as an isolated farm (wick) out in what would originally have been marshy ground (fen).

Barnby Dun is another Danish *-by* name with the addition of Dun (= River Don on whose banks it stands) to distinguish it from Barnby Moor (Notts) about twelve miles away.

Armthorpe contains another place-name element common in the eastern part of the county (e.g., Hexthorpe, Thorpe in Balne, Thorpe Salvin) showing the importance of Danish settlement in the area. Thorpe means a small settlement established a short distance away from an existing one (e.g., Scawsby and Scawthorpe, which are only three-quarters of a mile apart).

Bessacarr does not mean some kind of marsh (carr from Old Norse *kjarr* as in Deepcar and Elsecar) but is derived from a grassy (*beos* = bent grass) plot of land (acre).

Micklebring means great slope from Old Norse *micel* (= big) and bring which is a corruption of brink as 'on the edge of'). Micklethwaite, a common West Riding surname, is from the same root and means big clearing (in woodland).

Wales is an Old English name and means 'The Welshmen', denoting an isolated Celtic settlement in an area otherwise dominated by Anglo-Saxons. Walton in north Derbyshire comes from the same root.

Handsworth and **Handsworth Woodhouse** provide an example of twinned settlements like Wentworth and Wentworth Woodhouse and Hatfield and Hatfield Woodhouse. Handsworth (worth = enclosure) is the parent settlement and Handsworth Woodhouse is the daughter settlement some way off in the surrounding woodland. Significantly, Handsworth is recorded in the Domesday Book in 1086 but Woodhouse was not recorded until 1200.

STREET AND ROAD NAMES

Streets, roads and lanes have been surfaced and re-surfaced for centuries, there will have been changes of direction, some slight others major, buildings have come and gone, but the names live on (Figure 3.6). They give us a sense of place and direction. Even Meadowhall Shopping Centre has its streets High Street, Market Street and so on to make us feel we are in a 'real place'. But it is the real names rather than the thought-up names that give a place its character. If only Truelove's Gutter and Goose-turd Green had survived from Tudor Sheffield!

It is very difficult to classify all street names satisfactorily. If we confine ourselves first of all to **streets that originated before 1750** we can classify them in at least fourteen different ways!

1. Different sizes and importance of streets: from most important to least important, medieval streets were called road, street, lane, walk and alley, just to mention the most obvious names. High Street means chief or principal street (found in Sheffield, Doncaster and 41 other smaller places).

The word street or road is often replaced by the Old Norse *gata* (gate) as already noted earlier in this chapter. One of the most interesting names is found in Rotherham - Narrow Twitchell, which is a narrow snicket off Hollowgate (hollow = sunken).

2. Indicating a direction: West Street and South Street (Sheffield); Westgate, Eastgate (Barnsley); Northgate (Tickhill).

3. Specific places to which they lead: There are 40 Church Streets, 27 Church Lanes and three Churchsides in South Yorkshire; St Sepulchre Gate (Doncaster, leading to a church of that name); Abbey Lane (Sheffield); Bridgegate (Rotherham); Spittal (i.e., Hospital) Hill (Sheffield); Doncaster Gate (Rotherham); Chapel Walk (Sheffield). Salt routes from Cheshire are commemorated by Salter Hill Lane (Stocksbridge), Salter's Way (Penistone), Psalters Lane (Rotherham) and Psalter Lane (Sheffield). Routes to burial places in churchyards are commemorated in Burying Lane between Hoyland and Wentworth (old church) churchyard. Priory Road beside Ecclesfield church was also formerly Burying Lane. Castlegate in Sheffield sounds medieval but was only given in 1930!

4. Specific uses: Pack Horse Lane (High Green); Packman Lane (Harthill); Packman Road (Wath); Waingate (Sheffield) - a wain was a wagon.

5. Named after inns and taverns: Hartshead and Angel St, both in Sheffield .

6. Cul-de-sacs: Blind Lane (lost, Sheffield).

7. Length, shape, steepness, general appearance: Broad Lane (Sheffield); Dog Leg Lane (Ecclesfield, lost); Hollowgate (Chapeltown and Rotherham); Sheffield has two Hollow Lanes.

8. Ethnic clusters: Frenchgate; Scotgate (both Doncaster).

9. Trades and industries: Baxter (= baker) Gate and Fisher Gate (Doncaster); Fleshgate (= Butchers' quarter) (Rotherham, lost); Furnace Hill (Sheffield); Tannery Street (Woodhouse); Change

Alley (site of Sheffield's first Stock Exchange); Pudding Lane and Baker's Hill (Sheffield, both lost).

10. Markets: Market Hill (Barnsley); Market Place (Doncaster). Shambles (butchers' quarter) Street (Barnsley); Cheapside (Barnsley; *ceap* is Old English for market). Haymarket (Sheffield) is a nineteenth century invention.

11. Streets leading to or across a common on the edge of a town: The Moor (Sheffield); Attercliffe Common (Sheffield); Moorgate (Rotherham).

12. Associations with trees and other plants: Figtree Lane, Holly Lane, Mulberry Street, Orchard Lane (all Sheffield).

13. Landowners or occupiers: Barker's Pool (Sheffield) - Adam Barker was a landowner here in 1333; Blonk Street - Blonk family, scissorsmiths, had a workshop there called Blonk Wheel.

14. Miscellaneous: Boggard Lane (Oughtibridge and

Figure 3.6. Three contrasting South Yorkshire street names. Boggard (ghost) Lane at Worrall; Narrow Twitchell (twitchell = snicket) in Rotherham and Aldrin Way (Buzz Aldrin, the astronaut) at Maltby. The Author

Penistone; a boggard is a ghost); Bole Hill Road (Sheffield) and Bole Hill Street (Eckington and Sheffield, a bole hill being an exposed westward facing hill where metal was smelted using the natural draught of south-westerly winds); May Day Green (Barnsley, where May Day celebrations were held); Kirk Balk (Hoyland; a balk was a narrow grassed path across a medieval open field, in this case the Church or Kirk Field).

The second half of the eighteenth century and the whole of the nineteenth century saw a spate of new building in the major towns of South Yorkshire and in the rapidly growing industrial settlements, and a new phase of street naming was initiated. Six clear groups of names can be easily identified:

1. Landowners: The great local landowners such as the Earl of Effingham, Earl Fitzwilliam, and the Duke of Norfolk were involved in laying out streets on their land. One of the best documented developments is the one in Sheffield on the former Alsop Fields belonging to the Duke of Norfolk. The new development (1771-78) in the form of a grid iron plan of new streets on the edge of the old town of Sheffield is easily recognised to this day because every street has a name connected with the Duke of Norfolk: Norfolk Street, Surrey Street, Howard Street, Eyre (the name of his agent in Sheffield) Lane, Arundel Street, Furnival Street, Charles Street, Earl Street.

2. Wellington, Waterloo, etc: There are sixteen Wellington Streets, Roads and Places in South Yorkshire; there is a Waterloo Road in Barnsley; and Blucher Street (Blucher was the Prussian general who fought with Wellington at Waterloo) in Barnsley.

3. Crimean War: Balaclava Road and Street (Sheffield); Inkerman Road (Darfield); there are six Alma roads/streets in South Yorkshire, but no Sebastopols.

4. Boer War: Mafeking Place (Chapeltown); Ladysmith Avenue (Sheffield); Kimberley Street (Sheffield); Bloemfontein Road and Street (Cudworth). In Conisbrough there is a row of houses all with names from the Boer War.

5. Victoria and Albert: There are 48 streets in South Yorkshire embodying the word 'Victoria', nineteen with 'Albert' and eighteen with 'Regent'. Leopold Street in Sheffield is named after Prince Leopold, Queen Victoria's son, who opened Firth College in the new street in 1879.

6. Politicians: Nineteenth century politicians are particularly well represented in Barnsley, reflecting its spectacular growth in the Victorian period: Eldon, Pitt, Castlereagh, Peel, Canning.

Because of the continuing rise in population, the trend to smaller households, improved public transport and private car ownership, and increased home ownership, housebuilding and the spread of settlement has been a major feature of the twentieth century. More houses have meant more streets and in some places planners and private developers seem to have run out of ideas for street names. Look out for the following types:

1. Flowers: e.g., the 'flower estate' in Sheffield - Bluebell Road, Daffodil Road, Clematis Road, Hyacinth Road...

2. Trees: e.g., 1970s private estate on Chapel Road, Chapeltown - Acacia, Ash, Cedar, Cypress, Elm, Firtree, Hazel, Hornbeam, Redwood, Walnut, Willow...

3. Birds: e.g., private estate at Thorpe Hesley - Bittern, Curlew, Fulmar, Linnet, Kingfisher, Merlin, Sandpiper...

4. Areas of outstanding beauty: e.g. Athersley, Barnsley has Buxton, Chatsworth, Crich, Derwent, Hardwick and Monsal; and in Sheffield 8: Buttermere, Cartmel, Grasmere and Thirlmere.

5. Politicians: The labour party at Maltby: Attlee Close, Cripps Close, Hardie Close, Jowitt Close, Lee Close.

6. Poets and novelists: at Maltby again: Burns, Byron, Coleridge and Tennyson...; Conisbrough has Ivanhoe, Athelstane and Rowena from Sir Walter Scott's *Ivanhoe*.

7. Explorers: e.g., at Maltby again: Columbus, Magellan and Scott rub shoulders with Aldrin, Armstrong and Bonnington. At Charlton Brook (Chapeltown) Stanley Road leads to Livingstone Road.

8. Local worthies: e.g. Keble Martin Way at Wath (former vicar; botanist); Charles Ashmore Road at Norton (artist); Foster Way, High Green (John Foster was coroner, writer of sacred music including the well-known tune 'Old Foster'); Solly Street (Sheffield) (alderman); Kinsey Road and Cottam Road at High Green after a local headmistress and headmaster respectively.

9. Racecourses: Scawthorpe contains streets called Lingfield, Wetherby, Beverley, Teeside, Kempton ... And there is another modern estate named in much the same way in Mexborough.

10. Peculiarities: e.g. Barmouth, Falmouth, Lynmouth and Plymouth in Nether Edge Sheffield. Were these the whim of a builder with Welsh and West Country connections, or was the sequence based on repeating the names of places ending in -mouth?

What to read about place-names

K. CAMERON, *English Place-Names*, Batsford, 1996.

J. FIELD, *Discovering Place-names*, Shire Publications, 1984.

M. GELLING, *Signposts to the Past*, Phillimore, third edition, 1997.

I. S. MAXWELL, The Age of Settlement, pp. 121-137 in David L. Linton (ed) *Sheffield and Its Region*, British Association for the Advancement of Science, 1956.

K. H. ROGERS, *Vikings and Surnames*, William Sessions Ltd, 1991.

A. H. SMITH, *The Place-names of the West Riding of Yorkshire, Part I, Lower & Upper Strafforth and Staincross Wapentakes*, Cambridge University Press, 1961.

M. WALTON, *Street Names of Central Sheffield*, Sheffield City Libraries, 1977.

FARMSTEADS, HAMLETS AND VILLAGES

BETWEEN THE SIXTH and the eleventh centuries two major streams of colonisation from mainland Europe transformed the genetic make-up of the population of South Yorkshire, a new language was born and new cultural ideas in the shape of the Roman form of Christianity and the concept of English nationhood made their mark on the landscape.

SETTLEMENTS BY 1086
Anglo-Saxon raiders had been attacking the east coast of Yorkshire and penetrating up the rivers Tees, Humber and Ouse from the second half of the fourth century and this may have been the reason for the re-occupation of the Roman fort at Doncaster in the fourth century (see Chapter 7). 'Anglo-Saxon' is an umbrella term for colonists originating in northern Jutland (Jutes, who largely settled in Kent), southern Jutland (Angles), the coastal regions of northern Germany and Holland as far as the mouth of the Rhine (Saxons) and the North Sea coast of Germany (Frisians). South Yorkshire was settled largely by Anglians.

By the middle of the fifth century permanent Anglo-Saxon settlement was beginning to take place in the English countryside already populated by the Celtic-speaking native population, but Anglo-Saxon settlement did not take place in South Yorkshire until the seventh century. It is from this time that names of places were given in Old English (Anglo-Saxon) and this enables some idea to be formed of the mixing of the native Celtic peoples and the new arrivals. By and large the Anglo-Saxons adopted the Celtic (or pre-Celtic) names for the major rivers: Don, Dearne, Rother, Dove. They also commemorated the existence of some pre-existing native settlements in names such as Wales (farm of the Welsh or foreigner), Bretton (as in Monk Bretton meaning farm of the British), Rossington where Ross is the Celtic *rhos* (moor), Penistone where Pen is the Celtic *penno* (hill or height), and Ecclesfield and Ecclesall where Eccles is the Celtic *egles* (church). The most common Anglo-Saxon elements were *-ton*, *-worth*, *-ley* and *-field* meaning farm, enclosure, woodland clearing and treeless site respectively, as already discussed in Chapter 3. These have given us such well-known South Yorkshire place-names as Darton and Hickleton, Cudworth and Warmsworth, Barnsley and Bentley, and Sheffield and Hatfield.

Two hundred and fifty years later another colonisation from mainland Europe, this time from Scandinavia, added another people and another linguistic ingredient to South Yorkshire. These were the Danish Vikings who began to settle in Yorkshire about 875. Their settlements are recognised by such distinctive elements as *-by* (farm, hamlet or village as in Denaby and Maltby), *-thorpe* (daughter settlement as in Goldthorpe and Armthorpe) and *-thwaite* (woodland clearing as in Braithwaite and Hangthwaite).

By the time of the Domesday survey in 1086 most of the settlements in South Yorkshire that we know today were already in existence. Figure 4.1 shows the distribution of the Domesday settlements. Only in parts of the eastern lowlands and in the west are there gaps in the settlement pattern. This is largely explained by the presence of bogs and land prone to flooding in the east and the fact that the Domesday surveyors mentioned sixteen berewicks (hamlets) in Sheffield manor but did not name them. Five of the places named in the Domesday survey in South Yorkshire have never been satisfactorily

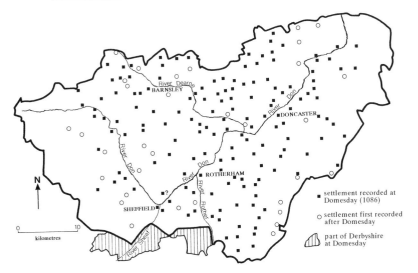

Figure 4.1. Settlements in South Yorkshire named in the Domesday survey, 1086.

located, but of about 160 that have, only one has completely vanished and is not named on modern maps. This is Wildthorpe, which was on the edge of the Magnesian Limestone escarpment near High Melton. Others are little more than names of single homesteads or halls such as Barnby, Stotfold, Bilham, Stancil and Wilsic. Frickley survives in the form of an isolated church surrounded by fields, and Hangthwaite, near Adwick le Street, is just a name on the map although there is a Norman motte and bailey castle and a medieval moated site nearby. However the vast majority of places named and described in the Domesday survey survived into the modern period.

What needs to be remembered is that the places that were in existence by 1086 were a combination of places or territories that might have been occupied since Iron Age times or before, while others would have been virgin sites or sites long abandoned until re-occupied by Anglo-Saxons and Danes.

SETTLEMENT SITES

Whether in the form of farms, hamlets or villages, these settlements were populated by groups of people who largely provided for their basic needs from their immediate locality, though having some links with neighbouring settlements. So why did our ancestors choose particular sites for their settlements? They needed water for themselves and their livestock, they needed land on which to grow crops, they needed grazing land, and they needed fuel and building materials. However they did not need these requirements in equal amounts, with the same frequency and with the same degree of access. Therefore each settlement decision would probably have been a compromise, where important decisions had to be made between a number of imperfect sites. Sometimes - perhaps usually - initial decisions proved to be unsatisfactory and settlement sites were moved over short distances. In the Pennine fringes in the west and in the lowest areas in the east good sites were less common than on the Coal Measures or on the Magnesian Limestone escarpment, and settlements were, and remain, more widely dispersed.

Settlements bordering the Dearne valley illustrate the general points made above (Figure 4.2). From Wombwell to Mexborough settlements are located on dry sites on gently sloping outcrops of Coal Measure sandstone. Water would have been obtained from wells. In the medieval period and beyond we know that the villages were surrounded by their open fields, again sited on the gently sloping sandstone with relatively fertile brown-earth soils. To the north of the open fields lay meadows (where hay was cut for winter feed) and riverside pastures. In these areas wildfowl would also have been hunted and fish caught in the River Dearne. To the south of the open fields lay the commons and woods providing pasture, and wood and timber for fuel and building materials.

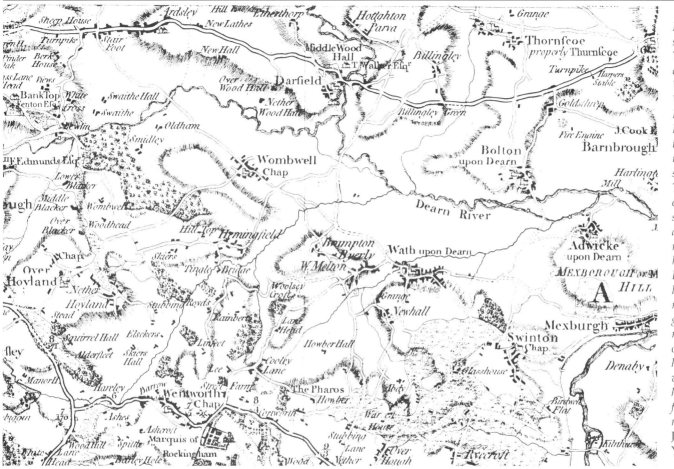

Figure 4.2. Settlement sites in the Dearne valley. The former farming communities of Wombwell, Brampton, Wath upon Dearne, Bolton upon Dearne and Darfield all made use in the past of the varied natural resources in their surrounding territories. The villages were sited on outcrops of sandstone and surrounded by their arable fields on reasonably well drained land on the same bedrock. Beyond, in one direction lay the low-lying meadows and wet grazing lands beside the river Dearne, while in the opposite direction was higher land containing woodland, scrub and heath, providing pasture, fuel and building materials. Thomas Jefferys, map of Yorkshire, 1775

In the west of the county resources were not so rich or as widely distributed. There, settlements were concentrated in folds in the landscape and in the once wooded valleys called *dens* by the Anglo-Saxons as at Ewden, Agden and Rivelingden (as the Rivelin valley was once called). In the Humberhead Levels in the east, settlers had to seek islands of dry land in the boggy and marshy environment as reflected in names such as Fenwick (marsh farm), Moss (wet bog), and Almholme, Eskholme and Shaftholme (*holme* is the Old Norse word for, among other things, an island of firm ground in a marsh).

VILLAGE SHAPES

A perusal of maps of South Yorkshire before the nineteenth century such as Thomas Jefferys' multi-sheet map of Yorkshire of 1775 shows that villages came in every shape and size imaginable. Size can to some extent be explained by variations in the richness of resources. Those villages surrounded by territories containing good soils and a good mix of other essential resources could support larger populations than those less well endowed. Another factor restricting size was landlord power. Where most or all of the land in a particular township or parish was owned by one family, the village was often restricted in size. These estate villages are sometimes referred to as 'close' villages, as opposed to 'open' villages where land was in mixed ownership, in-migration was largely uncontrolled and building was less restricted. Wentworth, Wortley and Hooton Pagnell are good examples of 'close' villages - the first two with their main or only public house named after the chief landowner (*Rockingham Arms* and *Wharncliffe Arms* respectively).

The shape of villages is much less easy to explain. Although much rebuilding would have taken place since the early medieval period, the villages portrayed on maps such as

Figure 4.3. Extract from Thomas Jefferys' map of Yorkshire (1775) showing variations in village shapes and sizes to the east of Rotherham. Thurcroft and Wickersley are street villages, Maltby is a nucleated village and Stainton appears to have developed around a green. Whiston is a composite village, nucleated in shape in the west but extending eastwards along a single street.

Jefferys' displayed their medieval layout. Most writers on settlement history now believe that many villages were often re-sited and re-planned - sometimes more than once - as the population grew and as changes in which the land was worked took place. But why this should have given rise to such a multitude of layouts is difficult to understand. Basically villages in South Yorkshire can be divided into four types based on their shape before many were transformed by industrialisation: street villages, nucleated villages, green villages and 'composite' villages (Figure 4.3).

Street villages as their name suggests, are the simplest in arrangement, running in a linear fashion along both sides of a long village street. Classic examples of street villages survive at Wentworth and Hooton Pagnell. Sometimes street villages had back lanes, and these survive today at Hooton Pagnell. Before industrialisation and suburbanisation Mexborough and Rossington were other good examples of the linear layout. Nucleated villages, i.e., irregularly, but tightly grouped farms and cottages connected by a network of lanes were the most widely distributed before industrialisation, and were found throughout the county irrespective of topography and soils. They were grouped around ancient parish churches, castles, at cross roads and at fords and bridging points. Green villages had a central green and strongly suggest an element of planning, where the central green provided a place of refuge for humans and animals in troubled times. One of the clearest examples of a green village in South Yorkshire, before industrialisation engulfed it within Sheffield, was Attercliffe (Figure 4. 4). The fourth type of village based on shape is the composite village, which was also widely distributed in South Yorkshire and which incorporated elements of the other three types, so it could be a nucleated core with linear extensions, a linear green village or a nucleated village incorporating a village green.

Figure 4.4. *Attercliffe as shown on William Fairbank's map of the parish of Sheffield, 1795.*

Villages evolve, often slowly, sometimes quickly and this poses difficulties when trying to classify them according to their shape. The village of Hoyland Nether illustrates this. In 1771 before the enclosure of the village's open fields, the village was an interesting example of an irregularly shaped green village (Figure 4.5 (a)). By the 1790s, after enclosure, and the allocation of every square foot of common land, including the village green, to an individual owner, the village suddenly became a street village, with cottage gardens carved out of the former green and running down to the new village street (Figure 4. 5(b)).

THE IMPACT OF INDUSTRIALISATION

Over the last two centuries industrialisation in South Yorkshire

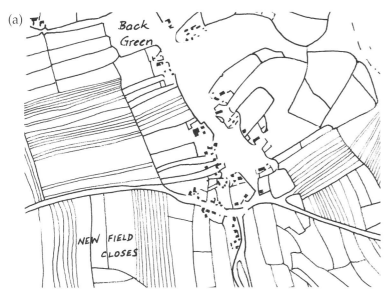

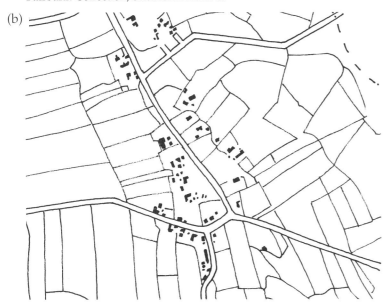

Figure 4.5. Hoyland Nether (a) before enclosure of commons, greens and open field strips in 1771, and (b) as shown on the enclosure award of 1791. Fairbank Collection, Sheffield Archives

has caused some villages to be engulfed by expanding towns, has resulted in others being enlarged and changed out of all recognition and has led to the creation of completely new industrial villages.

The major reason for the development of industrial villages in South Yorkshire has been the development of the coal mining industry, and this has given rise to dozens of pit villages. Some, particularly those associated with the exploitation of the concealed coalfield on or to the east of the Magnesian Limestone escarpment in the first two or three decades of the twentieth century, may last for at least another century in their present form. Others have disappeared completely within a century of their creation. Yet others still remain, but most of the the original buildings have been replaced.

In terms of their size, shape and internal design, South Yorkshire's colliery settlements are of five basic types.

1. Small colliery settlements, often in the form of a single or small number of terraced rows, often next to the pit gates, for example Long Row, Carlton, near Barnsley, and Westwood Rows at Thorncliffe, near Sheffield, now both gone. Colliery rows were typical of small-scale mining developments or the early stages of large colliery developments on the exposed coalfield in the nineteenth century. They were sometimes distinct units within larger settlements but were also often built away from existing villages, in the case of the Long Row at Carlton for convenience next to the pit, and in the case of Westwood Rows away from other miners' cottages because they were erected for blackleg miners during a lockout in 1869-70. The miners' rows at Elsecar (Old Row (see Figure 4.6), Station Row, Reform Row, and Cobcar Terrace) come into this category. Elsecar was a very small hamlet around a green before mining development.

2. Medium-sized colliery villages, again of nineteenth

Figure 4.6. Old Row, Elsecar, built c. 1795, the longest surviving row of coalminers' cottages in the county. The Author

century origin, largely unplanned, away from existing villages. Worsbrough Bridge, developed next to a branch of the Dearne and Dove Canal and the South Yorkshire Railway, is a good example of this type of pit village.

3. Large colliery settlements, in the form of small towns, with no overall plan developed over a long period in the nineteenth and twentieth centuries around the cores of pre-existing villages, for example, Mexborough, Wath, Wombwell.

4. Large colliery settlements that grew up over a long period in the nineteenth century, often with no overall plan, and built away from pre-existing villages. Parkgate, near Rotherham, a combined iron and steel making / colliery

settlement, eventually outgrowing its pre-existing neighbour Rawmarsh, is one of the best-known examples (Figure 4.7). Denaby Main, built between about 1865 and 1900 is another example of a nineteenth century self-contained colliery village, containing by 1900 about 1,500 colliery company-owned houses in barrack-like rows.

Writing about types 2, 3 and 4, Coates and Lewis in 1966, described them as 'unplanned, untidy, colourless and for the most part treeless.' They went on to say:

These are untidy and dirty landscapes. Domestic and industrial smoke, smells from coal-preparation plants, dilapidated pre-mining buildings, decaying terrace-houses, smoke-blackened buildings, garish colour schemes, unkempt gardens and allotments, prefabricated or improvised garages and acres of sheer dereliction and waste cannot fail to have an impact on the observer, shocking the sensitive, disgusting the idealist and fascinating the inquisitive stranger. (Coates and Lewis, p. 35).

Needless to say, there has been considerable improvement since 1966. Now there are no collieries whatsoever on the exposed coalfield west of the Magnesian Limestone escarpment where these settlements developed in the nineteenth century. The colliery buildings have been demolished, spoil heaps have been landscaped and planted upon, and the housing has undergone considerable improvement or been demolished and redeveloped.

5. Large planned colliery villages, all on the concealed

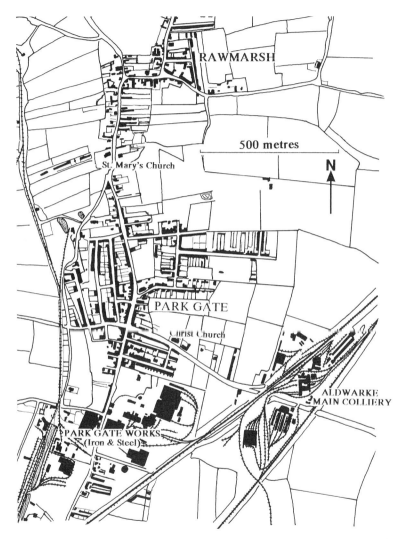

Figure 4.7. Rawmarsh and its industrial satellite, Park Gate, as depicted on the 1894 Six Inch Ordnance Survey Sheet 289 NE.

coalfield, all of early twentieth century origin, either engulfing pre-existing villages (e.g. Maltby) or growing up alongside but separate from a pre-existing village (New Edlington next to Old Edlington, New Rossington next to Rossington, New Bentley next to Bentley, Woodlands next to Adwick le Street). These are planned villages and often incorporate well laid out estates of geometrical design (Figure 4.8). They housed miners at widely spaced collieries (shafts were much deeper and much more expensive to sink on the concealed coalfield so the pits were designed to work much larger areas underground than their counterparts on the exposed coalfield) and so another characteristic of many of these villages is that they are separated from each other by large tracts of countryside, unlike types 1 (where they survive), 2, 3 and 4 on the exposed coalfield which merge into each other as in the Dearne valley between Wombwell and Conisbrough.

Not all colliery settlements fit into these five basic types, and in a number of cases on the exposed coalfield west of Rotherham, some former colliery settlements are very complex, having engulfed pre-existing pre-industrial settlements, spread in all directions and incorporated other colliery settlements into their built up area. In addition, some of the older colliery settlements on the exposed coalfield later acquired geometrically laid out estates (type 5) like the new colliery settlements in the Doncaster area.

THE IMPACT OF SUBURBANISATION

Every rural village in South Yorkshire has been affected by the suburbanisation of the countryside. What is meant by this term is the movement of urban dwellers into villages in the countryside and turning them into residential suburbs like those in neighbouring towns and cities (Figure 4.9). Even where new houses have not been built, farm buildings, schools, blacksmiths' shops and nonconformist chapels have

Figure 4.8. New Rossington, a planned colliery village on the concealed coalfield. 'Old' Rossington can be seen in the background. Aerofilms

all been converted to residential use. The rise in car ownership since the Second World War, allowing people to live in one place and work in another, is the major cause of this phenomenon.

It is possible to chart the change in village function from a rural village with most working adults in rural occupations to one where the majority leave the village every day to work elsewhere. This gradual change is shown in simplified form in Figure 4.10. Stage 1 shows the typical stage of development early in the twentieth century when car ownership was not common. The original village core containing the parish church, vicarage, working farms and farmworkers' cottages still dominates the scene. But the commuters have arrived. There may be the odd new house, both within the village core itself (an infill), or on the edge of the village (an accretion) and there may have been some early modifications such as knocking two small cottages into one. Stage 2 is typical of the 1930s. Car ownership had increased by that period and a wider cross-section of urban dwellers was considering the advantages of a 'rural' life style. At this stage ribbons of houses were built on the main roads leading into the village core. It was easier to provide services such as water, sewerage, gas and electricity along the main arteries in and between villages. After the Second World War this type of development was banned because of the fear that it would lead to 'sprawl'. From the 1960s onwards (stage 3), car ownership took off steeply, good sites in towns were increasingly difficult to find, home ownership was a greater possibility for everyone and certain villages were earmarked for housing development. Planners preferred villages to be filled out rather than extended along main roads and so a major feature of this stage is housing development in the form of estates, large (adjuncts) and small (more accretions). As land for development became scarcer in the 1980s and 1990s, accretions became more widespread with every nook and cranny within the permitted envelope of development being taken up by building companies. Conversions of farm buildings, chapels, vicarages and schools have remained as popular as ever. Not all villages have gone through these three stages. Some have infills and modifications and nothing else; others have no ribbons but large adjuncts and many accretions; some escaped the first two stages altogether and then the village core has been enveloped by one or two large estates.

Figure 4.9. Suburbanisation of the countryside. Photograph (a) shows the rural scene from the bedroom window in a village north of Sheffield in 1970. Photograph (b) shows the view from the same window in 1985. Joan Jones

(a)

(b)

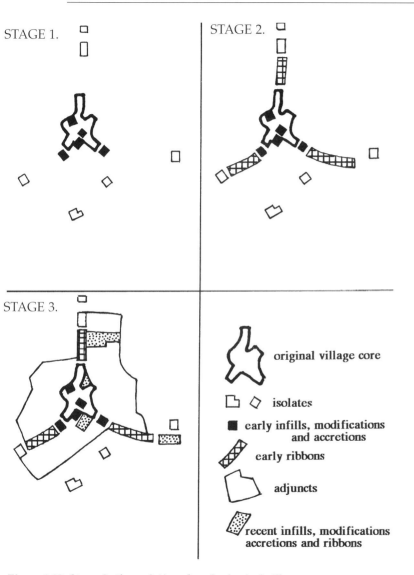

STAGE 1.

STAGE 2.

STAGE 3.

original village core

isolates

early infills, modifications and accretions

early ribbons

adjuncts

recent infills, modifications accretions and ribbons

Figure 4.10. Stages in the evolution of a suburbanised village.

What to read about South Yorkshire's farmsteads, hamlets and villages

COATES, B. E. and LEWIS, G. M. (1969) *The Doncaster Area: British Landscapes Through Maps 8*, Geographical Association, Sheffield.

HEY, D. (1979) *The Making of South Yorkshire*, Moorland Publishing.

JONES, M. (1999) 'Denaby Main: the development of a South Yorkshire mining village' in B. Elliott (ed) *Aspects of Doncaster 2*, Wharncliffe Publishing, Barnsley, pp. 123-42.

Places to visit

Interesting villages worth a visit when combined with a country walk and a pub lunch are **Wentworth** (estate street village), **Hooton Pagnell** (estate street village), **Grenoside** (loosely nucleated village suburbanised by conversions and infills, in a woodland setting), **Cawthorne** (estate village with attractive conversions and infills built over a long period), **Elsecar**, (an early nineteenth century industrial village), and **Fishlake**, (a largely unchanged village in the eastern lowlands with a beautiful Saxon church).

Some places have useful interpretive leaflets produced by the local authorities concerned such as *Grenoside: Woodland Village, Elsecar Heritage Trail, Elsecar to Wentworth Walk, Historical Guide*, and *Fishlake Heritage Trail*. These can be obtained from libraries and tourist information centres.

Sheets in the Alan Godfrey series of *Old Ordnance Survey Maps* are also useful when exploring local villages. The maps of *Thorpe Hesley and Scholes* (Sheet 289.01), *High Green and Thorncliffe* (Sheet 282.15), *Ecclesfield* (Sheet 288.08) and *Grenoside* (Sheet 288.07) can be highly recommended.

FARMED LANDSCAPES: FROM SAXONS TO SUBSIDIES

THE SEVENTH CENTURY Saxon settlers in South Yorkshire entered a land that had already been farmed for over four thousand years. Some areas had been farmed intensively, others only contained small and dispersed farming communities.

ANGLO-SAXON AND SCANDINAVIAN COLONISATION

What is perfectly clear from modern archaeological studies is that the traditional story of Anglo-Saxon settlement - of large numbers of colonists entering the area, causing the native population to flee westwards, and then establishing villages surrounded by open field systems - can no longer be sustained. Much still needs to be explained before a full interpretation can be attempted, but it is probably nearer the truth to think in terms of a relatively modest influx of settlers, occupying sites abandoned by earlier farmers, mostly at the scale of individual farms or small hamlets. These early Anglo-Saxon settlements were probably also eventually abandoned as new sites within a defined territory (possibly a later ecclesiastical parish) were colonised. Sites for settlement may have been available because of plagues which had reduced the size of the population substantially since the end of the Roman period. Danish Viking settlements were established in the ninth and ten centuries filling in gaps in the existing pattern of farms and hamlets, sometimes on virgin sites, sometimes on abandoned sites.

Variations in the agricultural environment and intensity of previous agricultural exploitation are reflected in the names given to places by the Anglo-Saxons and the later Scandinavian settlers. Figure 5.1 shows the Old English and Old Norse place-names in South Yorkshire indicating woodland and woodland clearance. A minority are medieval in origin but most were recorded by 1086. Remembering what has been said about settlements moving about a given territory, these place-names probably refer to a small territory rather than a specific site. In many cases the Anglo-Saxon and Viking woodland clearance names must indicate large

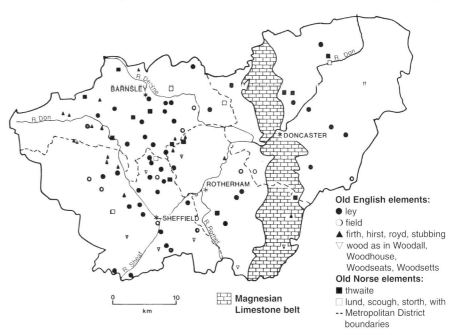

Figure 5.1. Old English and Old Norse place-names in South Yorkshire indicating woodland and woodland clearance.

clearings that had existed for many generations and they were merely being renamed in their own languages. The contrast between the Coal Measures and the other geological zones is striking. In the west woodland names are restricted to the eastern fringes of the Millstone Grit country where much woodland clearance had already taken place by the end of the prehistoric period. East of the Coal Measures, there are only three woodland names in the Magnesian Limestone belt, large parts of which had been intensively farmed since the late Neolithic. In the eastern lowlands large stretches were seasonally flooded and woodland names are absent over large areas. In complete contrast there are more than 80 woodland and woodland clearance names on the Coal Measures, suggesting that woodland was still a substantial component of the landscape or a powerful recent memory. By the time of the Domesday survey in 1086 the woodland cover in the county as a whole had been reduced to 13 per cent of the land area, but variations within the county were still marked - the figures for what are the present Barnsley and Rotherham metropolitan districts were about 17 per cent; for Sheffield it was 22 per cent, and for Doncaster only 9 per cent.

MEDIEVAL FARMS AND FIELDS

At some time between the ninth and thirteenth centuries, probably in the second half of this period in South Yorkshire, villages surrounded by communally farmed fields made their appearance in the English countryside. The Domesday Book in 1086 (see Chapter 4) which gives the names of most of today's villages and towns is more likely to be describing territories containing a number of separate dispersed farms rather than nucleated villages. Moreover, when villages did come into existence they were not found everywhere. They developed in the more agriculturally suitable areas which could support large populations. Where conditions were less propitious,

dispersed single farms and hamlets tended to continue to dominate the landscape, but hamlets often had one open field.

What prompted the reorganisation of substantial parts of the countryside into villages and hamlets with communally worked farmland as opposed to privately farmed land around individual farmsteads is unclear. Some writers consider that rapid population growth was the cause; others put more emphasis on inheritance patterns which meant that farms became increasingly fragmented.

Whatever the trigger was, by the thirteenth century, villages with two, three or even as many as six open fields, and hamlets with one or two open fields, were widespread in South Yorkshire from Carlecotes and Midhope in the west to Thorne and Hatfield in the east. Single farmsteads or hamlets with their surrounding irregularly shaped enclosed fields and extensive commons were the norm only in the area to the west of Sheffield and in parts of the eastern lowlands, and even there small open fields existed as part of a complex pattern of settlement and farm organisation. These varying arrangements are still fossilised in the settlement and field patterns in the modern landscape as shown in Figures 5. 2 (a) and 5.2 (b).

Figure 5.2 (a) shows the area between Oughtibridge and Dungworth to the west of the upper Don valley partly in Millstone Grit country and partly on the Lower Coal Measures, rising in places to 353 metres with many steep slopes. It is a district of hamlets and single farms, and although there were open fields at Bradfield and Dungworth in the medieval period, it is the mosaic of small and medium-sized, irregularly shaped, walled fields that has survived, some possibly originating as early as the Iron Age, others having been taken in from the waste (scrub woodland, gorse covered heath, heather moorland) in the medieval period and beyond. There is much documentary evidence of this process (called 'assarting' in the medieval period) in this area in the fourteenth

(a)

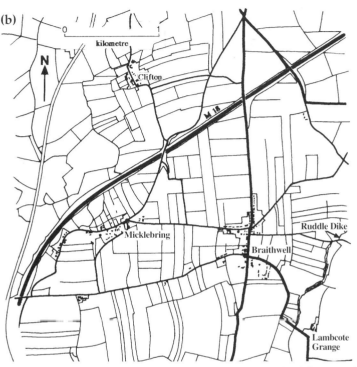

(b)

Figure 5.2. *(a) Field patterns in the Bradfield and Dungworth areas west of Sheffield.*

(b) Field patterns around Braithwell, Micklebring and Clifton in the Magnesian Limestone belt.

and fifteenth centuries. Figure 5.2 (b) shows the parish of Braithwell and surrounding area in the Magnesian Limestone belt. The settlement and field patterns are quite different from those shown in Figure 5.2 (a). Most settlement is concentrated in villages: Braithwell itself, Micklebring and Clifton. To the south of Micklebring and to the south and east of Braithwell the sinuous boundaries of medieval open field strips and furlongs (see below) are still preserved in the modern hedged field boundaries.

THE OPEN FIELD SYSTEM OF FARMING

There was no one universally adopted system of open field farming. Regional variations evolved, each having their own peculiar set of rules, varying over time, overseen and implemented by a manorial court or village assembly. Fully developed open field systems, as has already been pointed out, were more likely to have been widely adopted and been longer lasting in the eastern half of the Coal Measures and in the Magnesian Limestone belt, than further west or east.

The open field farming system had four essential

components: village closes, open arable fields, meadows and commons or waste. The village closes were small enclosed fields attached to the dwellings in the village and were called tofts where they included buildings and crofts when they did not. In a fully fledged open field township these would be the only areas of privately worked land. Beyond the village closes would be a number of large unfenced arable fields from one to as many as six or seven but usually between two and four. In a mature open field township the open field strips were individually owned but ploughed and harvested on a communal basis and the fields were communally grazed after the harvest. The fields were divided into compartments called furlongs, flatts or shotts. These were further subdivided into strips (or selions or lands). The strips and furlongs did not have straight boundaries, they were usually curved, forming a reverse S shape. This is because of the need to turn the plough team (usually oxen in the medieval period) at the end of the ploughed strip (called the headland). Because the plough turned the sod inward, each strip formed an elevated ridge separated from the the next one by a furrow. The ridge and furrow pattern can still be seen in fields put down to grass after the break up of the open field system (Figure 5.3). Beyond the open fields, often on low-lying damp ground, were the meadows where hay was cut for winter feed and which also provided pasture ground. Occupying the least favourable land for cultivation were the commons, providing pasture, especially in spring and summer when grazing was not allowed in the open fields and meadows, firewood, turf and constructional timber.

Figure 5.3. Ridge and furrow.

OPEN FIELD SYSTEMS IN DECLINE

A close inspection of a survey made in the late eighteenth century of Hoyland Nether, between Sheffield and Barnsley, reveals the complexity of the organisation of the farmed landscape resulting from the evolution of an open field system in the medieval period and its subsequent decline. Figure 5.4 shows the township (it was one of four townships making up the parish of Wath) in 1771. The village of Hoyland Nether itself was a straggling green village as already shown in Figure 4.5. Besides the village, there were four hamlets in the township: Upper Hoyland (A), Hoyland Lane End (B), Harley (C) and Elsecar (D). Between these hamlets stood nine dispersed farmsteads. The intriguing question that can be asked, but never satisfactorily answered, is: were the hamlets and dispersed farms relics of the settlement pattern before the development of open field farming and the development of Hoyland Nether as the main settlement, or were they, in part at least, the result of a pattern of dispersal initiated by the breakdown of the open field system?

The field pattern was very complicated. Surrounding the village, beyond the small fields (crofts and tofts) attached to the farmhouses, and occupying about 40 hectares, were the remnants of the open fields: Nether Field lay to the east of the village; Church Field (also known as Old Field and Lowe Field) lay to the west of the village; and to the south of Church Field was New Field. The names of the fields suggest a growth from a one to a three field system. Each field was divided into furlongs separated by grassed paths (balks) and the furlongs were divided into strips or lands as they were called. By 1771 the open field system was in terminal decline and instead of single strips, there were many bundles of strips, resulting from exchange and consolidation. Other strips had been taken out of the open fields altogether and fenced. These were called closes, examples of which can be clearly seen at X on Figure 5.4.

Beyond this compact central area lay a large area of fields of various shapes and sizes, all in private ownership by 1771. Some of these, bearing the name *ing*, represent the meadows that were originally an integral part of the open field system. Many others have the name *royd* (clearing in woodland), a common name in South Yorkshire for assarts reclaimed from the commons in the medieval period. Some regularly shaped fields around the hamlets of Upper Hoyland, Harley and at Alderthwaite Farm carried the field name *flatt*, an alternative name for a furlong, suggesting the possible former existence of open field land associated with these minor settlements. There were also 88 acres of woodland, owned by the major landowner and managed as coppices-with-standards (see Chapter 6). Finally, there were 150 hectares of inter-connected areas of common land, the largest area, covering 85 hectares, being Hoyland Common or the Great Moor.

ENCLOSURE OF OPEN FIELDS AND COMMONS

The break up of the open field system was under way in some localities before the end of the medieval period and there was much enclosure in the Tudor period. By 1600 nearly half of open field England was enclosed and by 1700 the figure was 75 per cent. Most of this was by agreement. By the middle of the eighteenth century with a rising population, rising prices for agricultural products, agricultural innovation and increasing regional specialisation, there was a movement to enclose the remaining open field land and associated meadows and commons. With complete enclosure farmers were free to experiment with new crops, new rotations and improvements such as under draining. This last round of enclosure was achieved by thousands of private acts of parliament, whereby opponents of enclosure could be defeated if the bill had the support of the owners of 75-80 per cent of the land. This was the so-called 'parliamentary enclosure' with most acts being

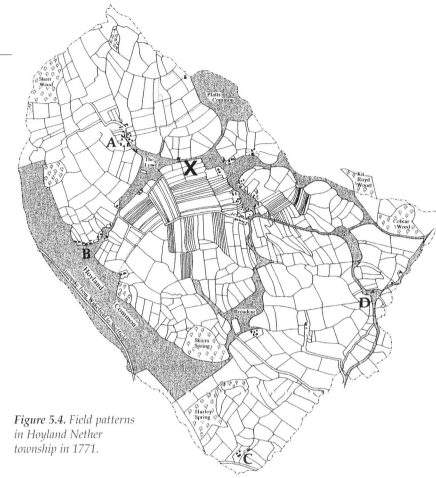

Figure 5.4. Field patterns in Hoyland Nether township in 1771.

passed in the period 1750-1830. Commissioners were appointed, the land was surveyed, and allotted to owners on the basis of land held in the common fields and their common rights. In the open fields exchanges took place to make reasonably sized holdings, and if substantial acreages were involved new farms were created, with new farmhouses. The new allotments, identified by their regular shapes, were enclosed by hawthorn hedges or walls. Tracks across commons were replaced by wide, straight roads.

Although cottagers without land lost their common grazing rights, most parliamentary enclosure acts were passed without civil disorder. However, the act to enclose the commons in Ecclesall, Hallam Moors, Rivelin valley, Crookesmoor and the village greens at Heeley, Newfield and Owlerton led to riots in Sheffield in 1791. These involved the release by the mob of prisoners from the debtors' gaol and the smashing of windows and the setting on fire of the library at the home of the vicar of Sheffield, one of the main beneficiaries of the act.

A second close inspection of Figure 5.2 (a) and (b) shows the impact of parliamentary enclosure in the two areas shown. In Figure 5.2 (a) the former Onesmoor to the east of High Bradfield can be identified from its regular field pattern of square and rectangular fields. The same is true of the former Loxley Chase described in 1649 as 'one great wood called Loxley the herbage common and consisteth of great oake timber'. After enclosure in the late eighteenth century it was divided into regular walled enclosures and crossed by straight roads, and the pattern has changed little in the intervening period. In Figure 5.2 (b) the former common to the north-west of Braithwell village is also easily identified from the regular field shapes. The remaining open field strips and the commons at Hoyland Nether had all been enclosed by 1796.

LAND DRAINAGE IN THE EASTERN LOWLANDS

Reclamation of land from marshland and land liable to seasonal flooding was a feature of settlement in the eastern lowlands from early times. In the medieval period it was most advanced in the clay lowlands to the west of the Don bounded by the River Went in the north (the present county boundary) and Askern in the west. This is reflected in the present landscape. The land is flat and nowhere more than six metres above sea level and the settlements, with the exception of Fishlake and the colliery settlements at Askern and Bentley, are

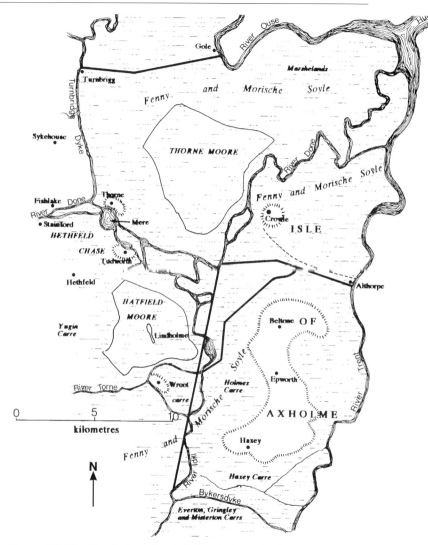

Figure 5.5. *The Humberhead Levels before drainage in the 1620s, and the main features of Cornelius Vermuyden's 1626 drainage scheme.*

hamlets and isolated farms sited on what were small, low islands in marshy ground. Place-name elements such as -ey as in Arksey (from the Old English for an island in a marsh), -holme as in Almholme (from the Old Norse for an island in a marsh), -lake and -fleet (both Old English words for a small stream) as in Fishlake and Trumfleet, and fen (marsh) as in Fenwick, all testify to the wet environment. The complex network of winding lanes linking the villages, hamlets and farms - there is rarely a direct route from one place to another - is also a result of the need to pass from one patch of dry land to another even if it meant a circuitous route. The fields are hedged, and there are many mature roadside and hedgerow oaks, ashes and willows, giving the landscape an enclosed atmosphere, and something quite unique in South Yorkshire.

Much of the land reclamation in the claylands must have been piecemeal and improved and amended over a long period. Changes were more dramatic in the area to the east of the modern A614 road and stretching across the county boundary to the River Trent and including the Isle of Axholme. Large parts of this area, much of which lies at about two metres above sea level, was a wilderness of marsh and bog as late as the early seventeenth century (Figure 5.5). A large part of it comprised Hatfield Chase (68,000 hectares), belonging to the Crown. The conditions in some parts of it can be gauged from the fact that when the last deer hunt took place in 1609 it is said that the royal party pursued 500 swimming deer in a flotilla of 100 boats. In 1626 King Charles I engaged the Dutch engineer Cornelius Vermuyden to drain the land. His scheme involved changing the course of the River Don so that it fed into Turnbridge Dike and then into the Aire, and by draining the staightened River Torne and the straightened River Idle into the Trent at Althorpe. One of the consequences of his work was increased flooding in the Fishlake and Sykehouse areas to the east and this led to the construction of the Dutch River to Goole.

As a result of Vermuyden's initial drainage scheme, later remedial work and the practice of warping (controlled flooding of land by tidal water to leave a layer of silt) this area is one of the most fertile arable farming districts in England. But its character is quite different from that of the claylands to the west of the Don. Here the landscape is more open, there are fewer trees and hedges, fields are larger, and farms dispersed.

RECENT CHANGES IN THE AGRICULTURAL LANDSCAPE

With certain exceptions - such as Vermuyden's drainage scheme or the parliamentary enclosures - countryside change before the second half of the twentieth century tended to be evolutionary rather than revolutionary. The last 50 years, however, have seen some of the most dramatic changes ever to take place on South Yorkshire's farms.

First, and perhaps most dramatically, the working horse has disappeared to be replaced by the tractor (Figure 5.6). This has meant that oats, grown for fodder for horses, has virtually disappeared (in 1997 there were only 250 hectares of oats on 86,000 hectares of farmland in South Yorkshire). More significantly, in the quest for greater efficiency in the mechanical age, fields have been enlarged in those areas where intensive arable farming has become almost a monoculture, which include large areas in the eastern half of the Coal Measures, more or less the whole of the Magnesian Limestone belt and large parts of the eastern lowlands. It has been estimated that since 1945, fuelled by central government subsidies and then by the European Union's Common Agricultural Policy (CAP), 240,000 kilometres of hedgerow have been grubbed up in England and Wales, creating prairie landscapes. In the central parts of the Coal Measures, opencast mining, in the 1940s and 1950s in particular, also played a significant part in removing old field systems and changing

Figure 5.6. Working horses at Rainstorth Farm, Ecclesfield, in the 1930s. The extinction of the working horse on farms and in industry over the last 50 years has meant the virtual disappearance of oats (their fodder crop) on South Yorkshire's farms. John Greaves

the face of the agricultural landscape in South Yorkshire (Figure 5.7).

The loss of hedgerows has not only created a much more open landscape in arable areas, where once mixed farming was more widespread and hedges an essential component of farm management, but has contributed, along with the almost universal use of herbicides and pesticides, to the increasing ecological barrenness of much farmland. Ancient hedgerows (i.e., those originating in the medieval period and before), and their accompanying ditches, banks and unploughed headlands, are the richest in shrub and tree species and are extremely important feeding, roosting and breeding sites for birds, mammals and a host of insect species. Some of the quintessential sounds and sights of the farmed countryside - singing yellowhammers and corn buntings, coveys of partridges, soaring skylarks, feeding winter flocks of redwings and fieldfares - are being threatened by the grubbing up of hedgerows. Hedgerow loss is also eroding the landscape evidence of the way our ancestors tamed the wildwood, heath and marsh and of our connection with the past. Walls are also important ecologically and historically and fortunately in the western areas, agricultural change has not resulted in the widespread destruction of field walls.

Other major changes in the appearance of the farmed landscape have resulted from specialisation, the sowing of new strains of wheat and barley and the introduction of completely new crops and land uses. Mixed farming has declined and farms tend to specialise in dairying, in raising sheep and cattle or just growing crops. In 1997 a third of South Yorkshire's farms were arable farms and they covered 57 per cent of the farmed area. There is now almost no autumn and winter fallow which provided spilt grain and other seeds for wildlife. Wheat and barley (together occupying 32,000 hectares in 1997) are overwhelmingly sown in autumn not spring, and

Figure 5.7. Map A shows field boundaries south of Wentworth village in 1854. Most were hedgerows with many hedgerow trees.

Map B shows the same area after opencast mining in the 1940s and 1950s. The area to the south of the stream was untouched by opencast mining and retains its mid-nineteenth century field boundaries. Most of the rest of the area has lost its old hedges, walls and hedgerow trees and has a new field pattern, each field separated from its neighbours by concrete post and wire fences (shown by dotted lines).

are much shorter stemmed than in the past to ease combine harvesting. Grass is still an important crop on dairy and mixed farms, but hay making is virtually a thing of the past. Grass is now cut earlier and made into silage. New crops include sugar beet which is widely grown in the eastern lowlands, the ubiquitous bright yellow oilseed rape (grown on more than half of the arable farms), maize (or Indian corn) grown to be silaged or fed straight to cattle, flax (these are the pale blue fields) and the most recent newcomer, short rotation coppice

(fast growing willow to feed the new wood-using power station which is being built at Eggborough in West Yorkshire). Pick-your-own soft fruit farms are now well established everywhere, and such has been the demand for paddocks for riding horses and ponies that Professor Alice Coleman invented the land use category 'horsiculture' for her land use survey of the British Isles.

The most unusual new 'crops' are self sown; they are the uncultivated fields of weeds representing 'Set-Aside' land - land on which farmers are paid not to grow crops in order to reduce the food mountains that have grown as a result of subsidised farming throughout post-war western Europe. Set-Aside land now accounts for nearly 3,000 hectares of farmland in South Yorkshire.

What to read about the farmed landscape

BYFORD, D. (1997), Open field farming in Fishlake and Hatfielt', pp. 87-110 in B. Elliott (Ed) *Aspects of Doncaster 1*, Wharncliffe Publishing.

COATES, B. E. AND LEWIS, G. M. (1966) *The Doncaster District*, British Landscapes Through Maps 8, Geographical Association, Sheffield.

GOODCHILD, J. (1997) 'The enclosure of Mexborough', pp. 199-208 in B. Elliott (Ed) *Aspects of Doncaster 1*, Wharncliffe Publishing.

HARVEY, G (1997) *The Killing of the Countryside*, Jonathan Cape.

HEY, D. (1979) *The Making of South Yorkshire*, chapters 11 and 21, Moorland Publishing.

NEWBY, H (1979) *Green and Pleasant Land?*, Penguin Books.

POLLARD, E., HOOPER, M.D. and MOORE, N. W. (1974) *Hedges*, (The New Naturalist series, 58) Collins.

RACKHAM, O. (1986) *The History of the Countryside*, chapters 8 and 9, Dent.

SYKES, S. (1993)'The patchwork quilt: Finding Dodworth's medieval landscape', pp. 225-247 in B. Elliott (Ed), *Aspects of Barnsley 1*, Wharncliffe Publishing.

TAYLOR, C (1977) *Fields in the English Landscape*, Dent.

WADE MARTINS, S. (1995) *Farms and Fields*, Batsford.

Places to visit

Rivelin and Loxley valleys. Sheffield Countryside Management Unit has produced a self-guided trail leaflet called *Rivelin and Loxley Round Walk*. There are excellent views of the walled farmed landscape of part of the South Yorkshire section of the Dark Peak and Pennine Fringe, with hamlets and isolated farms, early enclosed fields and parliamentary enclosure fields.

Fishlake: Doncaster Recreational and Cultural Services Department has produced a self-guided trail leaflet called *Fishlake Heritage Trail*. The walk takes the visitor on a tour of the village and farmland in what is a largely medieval landscape of hedged fields and winding lanes.

Dating hedgerows: In 1974 Dr Max Hooper proposed that the more species of shrubs and trees in a hedge the older it was. This was based on the assumption that the oldest hedges were narrow strips of native woodland already containing several species, that when hedges were planted in medieval times several species would be used, and that the older a hedge was the more chance that new species would be added by seeds being brought by the wind and by animals. Additionally it is known that the majority of parliamentary enclosure hedges was initially composed of just one species, common hawthorn.

The rule has been tested in the field by numerous researchers and although there are problems if recent hedges are surrounded by old ones so increasing the possibility of colonisation, it provides a useful rule of thumb, especially if other information can be used to corroborate the general date of hedge planting (e.g., enclosure award maps).

Basically the formula is that one species of shrub (ignore bramble and ivy) or tree in a random 30 yards length of hedge is equal to 100 years. So a hedge with 1-3 species is likely to be a parliamentary enclosure hedge (1750-1900), a hedge with 4-5 species may be of Tudor or Stuart date (1500-1700), and a hedge with six or more species is likely to be of at least medieval date. *Try it out on your next country walk - but remember to take a good tree identification book with you.*

ANCIENT WOODLANDS

AN ANCIENT WOOD is one that is known to have been in existence since at least 1600. The significance of the date 1600 is that it was not until after that date that woods were planted. So any wood already in existence by that date may have been a descendant of the original wildwood (see Chapter 2). Ancient woods in a parish are likely to be much older than the parish church and are of considerable historical and archaeological interest. Figure 6.1 shows the surviving ancient woodland sites in South Yorkshire.

Most surviving ancient woods in South Yorkshire were managed as coppice woods from at least the medieval period until some time in the nineteenth century. In a coppice wood, in accordance with an overall plan, most or all of the trees are cut down close to ground level and from the stump or stool a number of poles grow vigorously. These are cut on a regular rotation (called the coppice cycle), usually about twenty years. Every time the coppice is cut more vigorous growth springs from the stool. In South Yorkshire the type of coppice management called coppice-with-standards was widely practised (Figure 6.2). In woods managed in this way a certain number of trees are allowed to grow as single stemmed trees and these are the standards. From a coppice-with-standards there are two products: timber from the standards and wood from the coppice poles. Coppice woods were an integral part of the local economy in the past. They provided constructional timber, charcoal and whitecoal for metal smelting, and bark for tanning leather; and they were the basis of a large number of crafts such as basket making, dish turning, furniture making, coopering and besom making.

The careful study of large-scale maps and SLOW walks around and through surviving ancient coppice woods at all seasons of the year can reveal a great deal about their history. The clues to look for are their names, their positions, their shapes, their boundaries, their internal man-made features, and the trees, shrubs, herbs, grasses and sedges that grow in them.

WOODLAND NAMES

Past cultures all had distinctive names for woods: the Celtic *coed* usually corrupted to chet or cet; the Old English *fyrth* (firth or frith), *graf* (grove), *hyrst* (copse or wooded hill), *sceaga* (small wood, now

Figure 6.1. Ancient woodland sites in South Yorkshire.

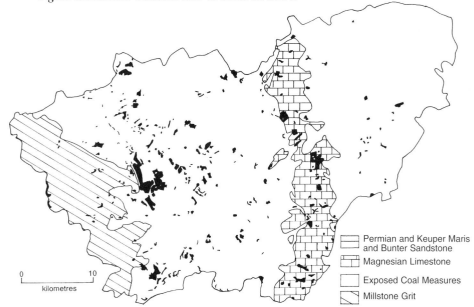

Permian and Keuper Maris and Bunter Sandstone

Magnesian Limestone

Exposed Coal Measures

Millstone Grit

0   10
kilometres

Figure 6.2. A diagrammatic representation of a wood managed as a coppice-with-standards. On the left is a part of the wood coppiced recently and in which regrowth is limited. On the right the underwood is several years old and has sprung from the stools to a height of five or six feet. Among the underwood are five standards of varying age. The wood is bounded by a bank (with a hedge) and ditch. On the woodbank is a pollard.

written 'shaw'), *wudu* (wood) and *spring* (coppice wood); the Old Norse *lundr* (grove), *skogr* (wood, written now as 'scough'), *with* (wood), *storth* (coppice wood) and *kjarr*, now written 'carr' (wooded marsh); and the Norman-French *copeiz* (coppice wood). Wood names that incorporate the names of villages, townships or parishes are also taken to be names of considerable antiquity, for example Ecclesall Woods and Hesley Wood.

The most common names of Old English origin are wood and spring. Wood is something of a problem. It was used over a long period of time, it was used to replace older names and it has continued to be used right up to the present time for new plantations. Spring is more useful in that it indicates coppice

management at some point in a wood's history, but it does not necessarily mean a wood is ancient. The term 'spring wood' was in common use until coppice management died out locally at the end of the nineteenth century. Among local woods bearing the name spring and known to be ancient are Low Spring at High Green, Wilson Spring between Birley Edge and Oughtibridge, Snaithing Spring in Ecclesall, and Ladies Spring Wood at Totley.

The Old English element *fyrth* is found in local documents in connection with wooded chases and commons. Rivelin Chase is referred to in Harrison's survey of the manor of Sheffield in 1637 as 'Revelin ffirth' and there is a document surviving from 1558 which refers to the 'Fyrthe of Westnall' in Bradfield which was a wooded common. There is a Frith Wood at Coal Aston and Greno Wood was once known as Grenofirth.

Old Norse names, like Old English names, are widespread locally. The wood that gave the Lundwood area in Barnsley its name was referred to in a document written in 1541 as the wood called *le high lunde*. The term carr is another Old Norse woodland name that has survived as a general place name, as in Deepcar. When applied to woods it described low lying woods bordering streams and rivers in which alders and willows predominated. There is a Carr Wood between Heeley and Gleadless in Sheffield and there is Holmes Carr Wood at Rossington. *Storth*, or storrs as it is usually now written, is another Old Norse element that is widespread. Besides being a wood name, it is used in stream names, names of hamlets and farms, and it is still a not uncommon surname in South Yorkshire. Its widespread distribution not only reflects the heavily wooded nature of parts of the area in the past but also the strength of Old Norse words in the evolving South Yorkshire dialect. The element is used in the name of the hamlet of Storrs between Stannington and Dungworth (where there is a Storrs Wood) and in Storrs Dike which is the boundary stream of West Wood, an ancient wood at Tankersley.

The element *copeiz*, of Norman-French origin, is also preserved in or near local woods, for example in Scholes Coppice near Rotherham and in Coppice Wood, Coppice House and Coppice Farm in the Rivelin valley.

Woodland names also reflect ownership, tenancies and functions. Prior Royd at Grenoside and Priest Wood and Prior Wood, which are old names for parts of Beeley Wood, strongly suggest ownership at some period by a religious house - in these cases by Ecclesfield Priory. Those woods that carry a personal name indicate owners (e.g., Lord's Wood (lord of the manor's wood) and woodwards (e.g., Wilson Spring named after Thomas Wilson the keeper of woods at Grenoside in the seventeenth century) or tenants as in Parkin Wood at Chapeltown where the Parkin family were tenants in the seventeenth century.

THE POSITIONS OF WOODS

Ancient woodland is often in remote places in a parish, in farthest corners and right on parish boundaries. It is also often on windswept hill tops, broad ridges and steep slopes and in narrow valleys, especially if they contain springs. As farms, hamlets and villages were established and woodland cleared for grazing and cultivation, the surviving woods acquired a scarcity value and were protected from grazing animals and managed as coppice woods. Naturally the more remote and difficult sites were more likely to survive.

A close look at the positions of ancient woods in Ecclesfield parish illustrates the point. Figure 6.3 shows the woods as they existed in 1810 before they were affected by mining and clearance for road development and settlement expansion. The large number of woods (25 in all) is unusual, as is the total woodland acreage of over 600 hectares. What is more remarkable is that almost all the woods have survived to the present day, if somewhat reduced in size, changed in shape, and usually either neglected or planted with conifers or non-native broadleaves.

Figure 6.3. Ancient woods in Ecclesfield parish in 1810. They all survive today.

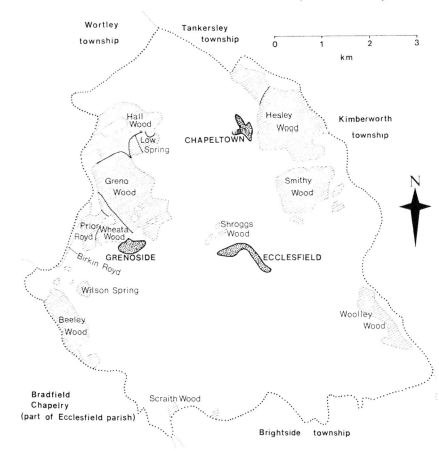

Looking at the parish as a whole, only the three small woods to the north of Ecclesfield village did not occupy parish edge locations. Besides their parish edge locations, many of Ecclesfield's woods occupy sites that would not have been amongst the most desirable for cultivation and settlement. Parts of Greno Wood rise to over 1000 feet and other woods are on very steep slopes. Birkin Royd seems almost vertical in places. Scraith, in Scraith Wood, means scree, a steep, boulder-strewn slope, and the early name of Scraith Wood was *Scryhcrest*, possibly a corruption of Scrith-hurst, reflecting its high, steep site above the middle Don valley. Other woods, although not occupying precipitous slopes, are on fairly steep valley sides as at Parkin Wood, Woolley Wood, Beeley Wood and parts of Prior Royd and Hesley Park.

Parish edge locations on steep slopes are repeated throughout the western half of South Yorkshire. West Wood and Thorncliffe Wood at Tankersley occupy steep valley sides above Blackburn Brook, and Hutcliffe Wood, Park Bank Wood, Old Park Wood, High Wood and Ladies Spring Wood all lie on steep slopes in the Sheaf valley in Sheffield. The element cliff in the names of local woods as in Thorncliffe, Hutcliffe and Shirecliffe (a large lost wood) is a reminder of steep slope locations. 'Hang Bank' in Hang Bank Wood at Gleadless in Sheffield simply means steep slope.

There are, of course, exceptions to these generalisations, and Ecclesall Woods, for example, although on a parish edge, lie on generally moderately shelving ground on unbroken terrain.

WOODLAND SHAPES

Many ancient woods are those parts of the original woodland cover, much modified by man, that remained when land had been cleared for cultivation, for pasture and for settlements. They are, therefore, 'left overs' that have been attacked by axe and saw over a very long period of time from different

directions by different cultures. Periods of rapid onslaught must have alternated with periods of inactivity as population growth gave way to stagnation, therefore lowering the demand for farmland, fuel, building materials and so on. It is not surprising, therefore, that old woods commonly have irregular shapes, unlike modern forestry plantations which tend to have straight sides and regular shapes.

Ancient woodland edges tend to be sinuous or zig-zagged with well marked peninsulas and bays like a rocky coast, as if giant bites had been taken from them. This unevenness is the

Figure 6.4. Ancient woodland shapes at Grenoside.

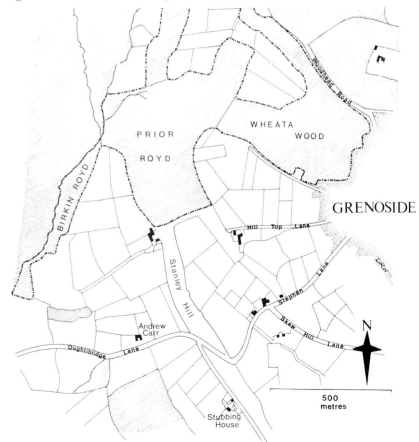

result of the unplanned, piecemeal clearing process, which in the medieval period was known as assarting and resulted in the creation of small irregular fields. Curving or zig-zagging woodland boundaries abutting on irregularly shaped fields with names indicating woodland clearance are widespread in the western half of South Yorkshire and can be illustrated by the adjacent woods of Birkin Royd, Prior Royd and Wheata Wood at Grenoside (Figure 6.4). It is as if a giant pastry cutter has been at work with the three woods representing the left-over pastry.

BOUNDARY AND INTERNAL EARTHWORKS

Woods, especially where there was much new growth as in newly coppiced woods, needed to be protected from grazing animals. Where outcrops of rock are absent over large areas, woodland boundaries were normally in the form of banks and ditches with the ditches on the outside. The higher and broader the bank and the deeper the ditch, the older it is likely to be. Thick hedges or wooden palisades often surmounted these banks and where trees grew on them they were often pollarded so that grazing animals in neighbouring fields could not feed on the new shoots. In areas where good building stone outcropped at the surface, stone walls took the place of banks and ditches. In South Yorkshire both ditched banks and, much more commonly, stone walls are found around old woods.

Among places where banks are to be found are Park Bank Wood at Beauchief, Low Spring at High Green, Rollestone Wood at Gleadless, Tinsley Park, and Canklow Wood. At Smithy Wood, at Thorpe Hesley, freestanding stone walls and walls built into natural banks have survived round the woodland. Figure 6.5 shows a particularly elaborate woodland boundary fence around Rockingham Wood on the Wentworth estate.

Earthworks in the form of depressions, ditches and banks also occur inside ancient woods. They may tell us something of the economic activities connected with a particular wood or they may confirm that the original wood was cleared at an early date for settlement or cultivation or some other economic activity and then allowed to revert to woodland.

Large coppice woods were sub-divided for management purposes and as the coppice poles in the various compartments were at different stages of development,

Figure 6.5. *Deep boundary ditch and revetted wall surrounding Rockingham Wood on the Wentworth estate.* The Author

animals may have been allowed in some parts of the wood and not others. In such circumstances internal walls, hedges or ditched banks with hedges or walls were necessary. Ecclesall Woods were subdivided into as many as twenty smaller coppices at various times and today some of the internal boundaries can be detected by the winding low banks within the wood (not to be confused with the equally numerous artificial drainage channels) which once supported walls and hedges.

Ecclesall Woods also contain more than 80 mysterious depressions, which also occur in Gillfield Wood at Totley, the Beauchief woods and the Gleadless valley woods. These depressions are four to five metres in diameter and have spouts at one end. They are mostly, but not always, on sloping ground near streams. Documentary evidence suggests that they were kilns in which whitecoal was prepared. This was kiln dried wood used as the fuel in water-powered lead smelting hearths between about 1575 and the mid-eighteenth century. Sites levelled for charcoal stacks (called charcoal platforms or pitsteads) are more difficult to identify and depend upon finding accumulations of charcoal and evidence of nearby temporary habitation. Careful searching has revealed substantial numbers of charcoal platforms in South Yorkshire's ancient woods.

Evidence of mining for both coal and ironstone, and of quarrying for stone may also be found in local woods. Evidence of past mining activity on the exposed coalfield is usually in the form of large shale mounds with central depressions. These mark the locations of former bell pits (see Chapter 11).

Many older earthworks also survive in some local woods and suggest that although the woods may be ancient they are unlikely to be direct descendants of the primaeval wildwood. In Scholes Coppice, for example, there is an Iron Age fort (see Chapter 7). It is unlikely that the defenders would want to be surprised by attackers creeping up on them through a wood. The wood, therefore, seems to have regenerated after the fort was abandoned. In Wheata Wood at Grenoside, Wombwell Wood, Canklow Wood in Rotherham and Edlington Wood, early settlement sites and field systems have been discovered, suggesting the woodland in the vicinity was cleared at an early date and then regenerated after the sites were abandoned.

ANCIENT WOODLAND TREES AND SHRUBS
The most widely distributed tree is the oak, usually the sessile oak in the west and central areas and the common or pedunculate oak (*Quercus robur*) in the east and south. The oak was the most important tree of local coppice woods, providing the most sought-after timber from the standards, and bark for tanning from both the standards and the underwood. The underwood was also used in coopers' work, basketwork and cleft paling making. Today oak is equally highly valued by conservationists because it supports over 250 species of insects which in turn attract a great variety of insectivorous birds.

It has already been pointed out that many ancient woods are on sloping ground, usually valley sides. On the higher slopes, where soils are shallow and nutrients have been washed out, rowan or mountain ash (*Sorbus aucuparia*) grows among the generally small oaks. The rowan was long thought to have magical properties and its local name was witchin or wiggin (bewitched). Birch, of which there are two native species, silver birch and downy birch, grows among the oaks and rowans on the upper slopes.

On the lower slopes where the soils are deeper and richer, the oak trees are taller and grow mixed with ash and wych elm (if they have survived the Dutch elm disease of the early 1980s). At streamsides at the bottom of slopes where waterlogging occurs, alders and willows become common.

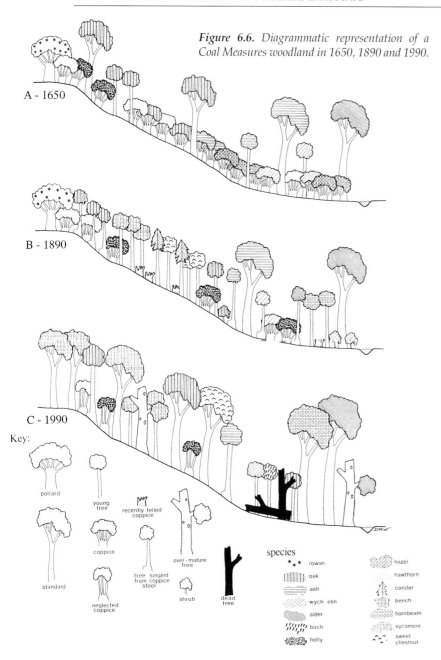

Figure 6.6. *Diagrammatic representation of a Coal Measures woodland in 1650, 1890 and 1990.*

Other less common native trees found amongst the more widely distributed oaks, rowans, birches, ashes, wych elms, alders and willows are crab apples, maples and wild cherries and, on the Magnesian Limestone, large and small leaved lime, and the very rare wild service tree *(Sorbus torminalis)*.

Beneath the tree canopy is a shrub layer composed of holly, hazel, hawthorn, (common hawthorn and the much rarer midland or woodland hawthorn *(Crataegus laevigata)*, elder, dog rose and guelder rose.

However, it should be remembered that none of our local woods is made up only of native trees and shrubs. Deliberate planting of broadleaved and coniferous trees and invasion from adjoining land by vigorous species such as the sycamore have changed them greatly. Figure 6.6 shows in diagrammatic form a typical wood on the Coal Measures in the western and central parts of the county as it might have looked (A) in 1650, (B) in 1890, and (C) at the beginning of the 1990s. In 1650 the wood is a coppice with standards with only native trees and shrubs. The main standards are oak, ash and alder. The underwood is mixed and there is a pollarded rowan on the upper boundary. By 1890 the wood has undergone a significant change. Coppicing is in decline because of loss of markets and the wood is being converted to a mixed plantation by singling the coppice and planting in the gaps where timber trees have been removed. Conifers have been introduced to produce a crop to be harvested within 30-50 years, and hornbeams, chestnuts and beeches - trees not native to South Yorkshire - have been planted for ornament and for timber. By 1990 the wood has changed character once again. It now belongs to the local authority and is no longer worked as a commercial wood. It is full of trees of roughly the same age. The majority are mature or over mature and form a dense canopy. This results in relatively little light reaching the woodland floor and consequently there is only a sparse shrub layer, a totally

Figure 6.7. Bluebell (Hyacinthus non-scriptus). The bluebell is the best known of the botanical indicators of ancient woodland, and probably the best loved of woodland flowers. What is perhaps not generally well-known is that it is only in the moist maritime climate of Britain and a few other places along the Atlantic coast of Europe that bluebells grow in profusion and carpet woodlands. We are the guardians of the world's bluebell woods. Joan Jones.

different situation from the one in 1650 when the felling of timber and the cutting of coppice was a regular activity. Other obvious differences between the mid-seventeenth and late-twentieth century wood are the presence in the latter of decaying trees, a wider variety of species including invasive sycamore, and dead and dying elms affected by Dutch elm disease.

Thankfully, more and more local woods are being actively managed again and the award of a £1.5M Heritage Lottery Grant in 1999 to manage 35 ancient woods in Sheffield, Rotherham and Barnsley is a welcome development.

WOODLAND HERBS, GRASSES AND SEDGES

One of the most striking features of ancient woods, and one which distinguishes them from recently established woods and plantations, is the rich and varied ground flora. One of the greatest delights of visiting old woods is to see the shafts of sunlight on carpets of wood anemones in April and bluebells in May (Figure 6.7). A walk through a coniferous plantation gives no such pleasure. It is dark and the ground is covered only in needles.

Ecologists believe that certain flowers (herbs), grasses, sedges and woodrushes are either restricted to or are rarely found outside ancient woods. They are called botanical indicator species. This belief is based on the notion that the slowest colonisers, particularly those that usually spread vegetatively rather than by seed, will only be found in long-established woodland sites.

A list of flowers, grasses, sedges and woodrushes believed to be strongly associated with ancient woodland in South Yorkshire is given in Figure 6.8. The list contains many common species. **Try it out in your local wood.** If there are substantial numbers (say more than ten) of indicator species, and the wood appears to be ancient from historical and

HERBS_____

Barren strawberry (*Potentilla sterilis*)
Bluebell *(Hyacinthus non-scriptus)*
Broad-leaved helleborine (*Epipactis helleborine*)
Bugle (*Ajuga reptans*)
Climbing corydalis (*Corydalis claviculata*)
Common cow-wheat (*Melampyrum pratense*)
Dog's mercury (*Mercurialis perennis*)
Early-purple orchid (*Orchis mascula*)
Golden-saxifrage (*Chrysosplenium oppositifolium*)
Greater stitchwort (*Stellaria holostea*)
Green hellebore (*Helleborus viridis*)   E R
Hairy St John's-wort (*Hypericum hirsutum*)
Lily-of-the-valley (*Convallaria majalis*)   E
Nettle-leaved bellflower (*Campanula trachelium*)   E
Pale wood violet (*Viola reichenbachiana*)
Perforate St John's-wort (*Hypericum perforatum*)
Pignut (*Conopodium majus*)
Primrose (*Primula vulgaris*)   E
Ramsons (*Allium ursinum*)
Sanicle (*Sanicula europaea*)
Slender St John's-wort (*Hypericum pulchrum*)
Square stalked St John's-wort (*Hypericum tetrapterum*)
Sweet woodruff (*Galium odoratum*)
Townhall clock (*Adoxa moschatellina*)
Toothwort (*Lathraea squamaria*)   E
Trailing St John's-wort (*Hypericum humifusum*)
Water avens *(Geum rivale)*   R
Wild strawberry (*Fragaria vesca*)
Wood anemone (*Anemone nemorosa*)
Wood forget-me-not (*Myosotis sylvatica*)
Wood horsetail (*Equisetum sylvaticum*)
Wood-sorrel (*Oxalis acetosella*)
Wood speedwell (*Veronica montana*)
Yellow archangel (*Lamiastrum galeobdolon*)
Yellow pimpernel (*Lysimachia nemorum*)

GRASSES, SEDGES & WOODRUSHES_____

Great wood-rush (*Luzula sylvatica*)
Hairy wood-rush (*Luzula pilosa*)
Pale sedge (*Carex pallescens*)   R
Pendulous sedge (*Carex pendula*)   R
Remote sedge (*Carex remota*)
Wood-sedge (*Carex sylvatica*)
Wood small-reed (*Calamagrostis epigejos*)   E R
Wood barley (*Hordelymus europaeus*)
Wood melick (*Melica uniflora*)
Wood millet (*Milium effusum*)

_____

E = found in east only, especially on Magnesian Limestone; R = rare.

landscape evidence then all the factors taken together prove conclusively that the wood is ancient. However, if documentary and landscape evidence suggests a site is not ancient, the occurrence of a few indicator species cannot be taken to mean that it really is an ancient wood. Whatever the outcome, identifying and listing the flowers, grasses, sedges and woodrushes adds to the enjoyment of a woodland walk.

Woodland plants, whether or not they are indicators of ancient woods, are adapted to the varied and changing conditions in woods. Grasses and sedges take advantage of woodland glades, rides, ditches and banks. Some flowering plants, called pre-vernal (before spring), come into flower before the trees come into leaf. Wood anemone, dog's mercury, and primrose come into this category. Another group of plants, including common cow-wheat, toothwort and some orchids, live partly off food obtained from decomposing litter or the roots of other plants.

One of the greatest pleasures of visiting a coppice wood is to see the explosion of flowering plants following the cutting of the coppice. In the first summer after the cutting of the coppice to ground level, the ground vegetation makes vigorous growth in the intense sunlight, and in the succeeding few springs and summers there are spectacular carpets of colour until the rapidly growing coppice and coppicing 'weeds' such as thistle, rush and willowherb reduce the sunlight reaching the woodland floor and suppress the ground vegetation. The increasing number of local woods that are being managed (thinning, coppicing and glade creation) can be expected to have a much more varied display of spring flowers than at any time within living memory.

Figure 6.8. *Herbs, grasses, sedges, woodrushes strongly associated with ancient woods in South Yorkshire.*

What to read about ancient woods

JONES, M. (1984) Woodland Origins in a South Yorkshire Parish, *The Local Historian*, 16, 73-82.

JONES, M. (1993) South Yorkshire's Ancient Woodland: the Historical Evidence. In P. Beswick and I. D. Rotherham (Eds) *Ancient Woodlands: the Archaeology and Ecology, a Coincidence of Interest,* Landscape Conservation Forum, pp. 26-48.

JONES, M. (1993) *Sheffield's Woodland Heritage.* 2nd edition, Green Tree Publications.

JONES, M. (1995) *Rotherham's Woodland Heritage,* Rotherwood Press.

JONES, M. (1998) The rise, decline and extinction of spring wood management in South-West Yorkshire. In C. Watkins (ed) *European Woods and Forests: Studies in Cultural History,* CAB International, pp 55-71.

JONES, M. (1998) The Coal Measure Woodlands of South Yorkshire: Past Present and Future. In M. Atherden and R. Butlin (eds) *Woodland in the Landscape: Past, Present and Future,* Leeds University Press.

Rackham, O (1990) *Trees and Woodland in the British Landscape.* Revised Edition, Dent.

ROTHERHAM, I. D. and JONES, M. (Eds) (1997) *The Natural History of Ecclesall Woods, Part 1,* Wildtrack Publishing Ltd.

Places to visit

Anston Stones, Rotherham (SK535830). Large wood on Magnesian Limestone known to have been a coppice wood in Elizabethan times. Contains rare trees and rich ground flora.

Bagger Wood, Barnsley (SK304025). Ancient wood (first known record fourteenth century) on steep slope on township (Stainborough) boundary. Planted with trees not native to the site but still a lovely bluebell wood. Now owned by the Woodland Trust.

Bowden Housteads Wood, Sheffield (SK397868). An inner city ancient woodland first mentioned in 1332. Managed for the first time in 100 years in the winter of 1988-89. Leaflet available from Sheffield Countryside Management Unit.

Ecclesall Woods, Sheffield (SK325825). Sheffield's largest ancient woodland site at nearly 300 acres (118 ha). Magnificent bluebell wood. Contains many whitecoal kilns and charcoal platforms and a monument to a charcoal maker who was burnt to death in the wood in 1786. Coppicing experiments are currently taking place in the wood. Leaflet available from Sheffield Countryside Management Unit.

Greno Wood / Wheata Wood / Prior Royd, Sheffield (SK330950). Extensive area of ancient woods adjacent to a village that still had a clog maker and a basket maker at the end of the nineteenth century. Leaflet *(Grenoside: Woodland Village)* available from Sheffield Countryside Management Unit.

FORTS, CASTLES AND OTHER DEFENSIVE FEATURES

SOUTH YORKSHIRE IS DOTTED with forts, castles, fortified houses and linear earthworks ranging from the Iron Age to the seventeenth century. Other fortified places have been lost and others are known only from their distinctive place-names.

IRON AGE FORTS

These have already been mentioned briefly in Chapter 2. They represent centres of military strength in a period when England was divided into tribal territories and petty fiefdoms. Each one would have been surrounded by a farmed countryside whose inhabitants would have owed allegiance to the local chieftain and would have looked towards the fort for protection in times of unrest.

Eight such forts survive in South Yorkshire (Wincobank, Canklow, Langsett, Stainborough, Brierley Common, Roughbirchworth, Scholes and Carl Wark (but see below)) and

a ninth (Roe Wood in Sheffield), which was lost earlier this century, is well documented. In terms of location the forts are of three types: hill forts (Wincobank, Canklow, Langsett, Stainborough, Brierley Common), hill slope forts (Roughbirchworth, Scholes and Roe Wood) and promontory forts (Carl Wark). Some doubt still surrounds the date of construction of Carl Wark and it may have originated in the fourth or fifth century AD.

The Wincobank hill fort occupies a commanding position overlooking the lower Don valley near the present-day boundaries of Sheffield and Rotherham. It lies only at 160 metres above sea level but as the land slopes away steeply in all directions its presence is felt for several miles around. Wincobank Hill is a hogsback - a long, narrow hill - of Coal Measures sandstone, bounded on the north-east by the valley

Figure 7.1 (a). Wincobank hill fort: plan. Figure 7.1 (b). Wincobank hill fort: the external ditch. Joan Jones.

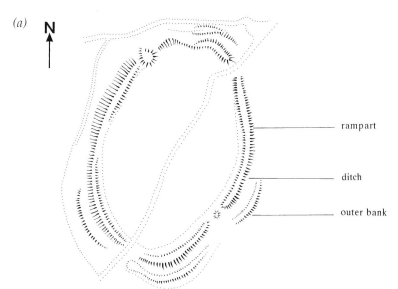

(a)

N

— rampart

— ditch

— outer bank

(b)

of the Blackburn Brook and on the south-west by a minor stream at Grimesthorpe. The result is a dry, easily defended hilltop with good all-round views. This made it an attractive location for occupation in prehistory.

The hill fort consists of an oval, defensive enclosure of just over one hectare surrounded by a single rampart with an external ditch (Figure 7.1a). The material from the excavated ditch has been thrown up into an outer bank. Today the grass covered rampart, which at one point rises 2.8 metres above the bottom of the ditch (Figure 7.1b), is more or less complete except for three breaks, through two of which - in the south-west and north-east - passes a long established track. The ditch and outer bank are absent along most of the western side of the fort and along the northern half of the eastern side.

Excavations by Sheffield City Museums in 1899 and 1979 have shown that the rampart was originally built as a stone wall 5.5 metres thick. The interior of the wall was filled with earth and sandstone rubble bonded together by timbers. It is not clear how high the original rampart was, but it would almost certainly have been topped by a palisade. No excavations have been made inside the fort and so whether there are any signs of occupation in the form of post holes for buildings is unknown. When the ramparts were excavated it was found that the timbers had been burnt and the stone rubble had been vitrified (i.e., fused into a glass-like substance by intense heat). The charring and vitrification suggest that the rampart was destroyed by fire. As has already been pointed out in Chapter 2, the charcoal was used to give a carbon date for the structure - 500 BC. More than 500 years later, Wincobank was probably re-occupied to check the northern advance of the Roman armies.

The hill slope fort in Scholes Coppice, at various times called

Figure 7.2 (a). Scholes hill slope fort: plan. Figure 7.2 (b). Scholes hill slope fort from the south. Joan Jones.

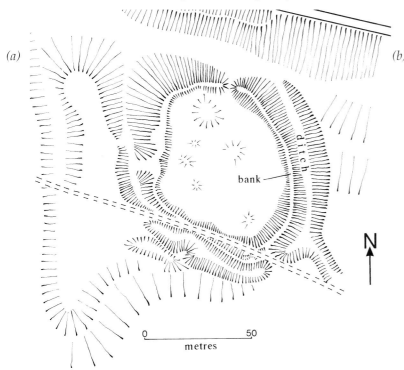

(a)

(b)

Caesar's Camp or Castle Holmes (Figure 7.2a and b) is in quite a different location from the fort on Wincobank Hill. Hidden today in the middle of a wood, it lies on the back slope of a sandstone escarpment, and is overlooked by higher ground to the south. The fort comprises an earthen bank with external ditch enclosing a flat area of about 0.25 hectares. The bank is 15 metres wide in places and rises between two and five metres above the ditch, which is also about 15 metres wide. There is no obvious entrance to the fort and it can only be concluded that it was entered by a bridge of timber construction. In 1991 an archaeological survey was conducted at the site. This work included the digging of a trench through the ditch and bank into the interior of the fort. The excavation showed that the bank incorporated layers of stone on top of a base of compressed clay. A post hole was found cutting into the clay base, suggesting that the stone and clay rampart was once surmounted by a timber palisade.

THE ROMAN RIDGE

Some way down Wincobank Hill from the hill fort is the remnant of another earthwork called the Roman Ridge or Rig. This is a linear earthwork in the form of a bank or a bank and

Figure 7.3. The Roman Ridge on Barber Balk Road, Kimberworth Park estate, Rotherham. The Author.

ditch, which stretches with breaks, for almost 16 kilometres along the northern side of the Don valley as far as Mexborough. In one stretch it is in the form of two banks more than 800 metres apart. At one point it runs at the side of a road on the Kimberworth Park housing estate (Figure 7.3). It is at its most impressive where it runs in an unbroken sequence through the southern part of Wath Wood. Despite its name it is not Roman. It was long thought to be prehistoric, and possibly built at the same time as the forts at Wincobank and Scholes. More recently, it has been suggested that it is of 'Dark Age' origin, built sometime between 450-600 AD after the collapse of the Roman Empire, possibly to defend the Celtic kingdom of Elmet (which stretched from Leeds to Sheffield) from the advancing Anglo-Saxons.

Another bank and ditch whose origins are equally mysterious is the so-called Bar Dyke, north-west of High Bradfield. This feature runs for about 400 metres in a north-east to south-west direction on the watershed between Ewden Beck and the stream flowing into Agden Reservoir.

ROMAN FORTS

Five Roman forts have been identified in South Yorkshire. One guarded the river crossing on the River Idle at Bawtry, another guarded the crossing over the River Torne at Rossington Bridge, another the river crossing on the Don at Doncaster, and a fourth near Robin Hood's Well to the east of Burghwallis. The fifth was also on the banks of the Don, this time at Templeborough, near Rotherham, facing the Brigantian hill fort at Wincobank. The Bawtry, Rossington, Doncaster and Robin Hood's Well forts were on the important Roman military route from Lincoln to Castleford and York. The sites of the Bawtry, Rossington and Robin Hood's Well forts have been identified by aerial photography. The Bawtry site, for example, discovered in the 1950s, was only a fifth of an hectare in size and guarded by three ditches.

The Doncaster fort, called *Danum* by the Romans, was the largest and most important of the four South Yorkshire forts on the Lincoln-York road. One reason for this is that it was also at the head of navigation on the River Don. It was established about 70 AD and covered just under 4 hectares. It was protected by a ditch and bank, and there was a civilian settlement beyond its bounds. The fort was abandoned when Hadrian's Wall was built (122-26 AD) but was re-occupied about 160 AD when a smaller (2.4 hectares) stone-walled fort was built, with a substantial civil settlement outside the walls. Danum was still occupied towards the end of the fourth century. Today little remains to be seen of Doncaster's Roman origins, but excavations in recent years, when urban developments have been taking place, have continued to provide extra information about its size and structure.

The Roman fort about which most is known and which has provided more artefacts than any other Roman site in South Yorkshire has disappeared completely. This is Templeborough which was buried beneath the Steel, Peech and Tozer steelworks complex in 1916-17.

The first Roman fort at Templeborough was established in 54 AD, as one of a series of forts built in order to support the pro-Roman Brigantian queen Cartimandia in her struggle with her anti-Roman consort, Venutius. This first fort was about 2.6 hectares in size and the garrison was about 1,000 strong. The buildings were of timber within a ditch and turf rampart. The fort was re-built about 100 AD in stone (stone-fronted defensive wall and stone administrative buildings) and again in stone in the fourth century. During the second phase of its occupation baths were built outside its northern perimeter and an industrial annexe, from which there is evidence of iron smelting and glass-making, was established outside the walls to the south-east. A simplified map of the Templeborough fort,

based on that drawn by Thomas May, who led an excavation in 1916-17 before it was lost beneath the steelworks, is provided in Figure 7.4. Objects from Templeborough may be seen in Weston Park Museum, Sheffield and the pillars from the fort's granary are preserved in the gardens at Clifton Park Museum, Rotherham.

THE SIGNIFICANCE OF PLACES CALLED 'BURGH'
In Old English, the language used by the Anglo-Saxons, the

Figure 7.4. *Layout of Templeborough Roman fort* After T. May.

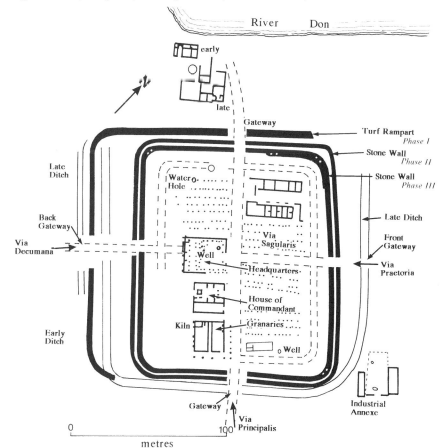

name for a fortified place was *burgh* which has been corrupted to *borough* or *brough*. South Yorkshire has a remarkable number of places with this place-name element: Burghwallis, Sprotbrough, Mexborough, Conisbrough, Barnburgh, Worsbrough, Stainborough, Kexbrough, Masbrough and Mosbrough (formerly in Derbyshire). These are all genuine old English *burgh* names. In Greasbrough and Munsbrough, the *burgh* element is a substitution, Greasbrough, for example, originally being Greasbrook. Templeborough, the name given to the site of the Roman fort south of the Don opposite Wincobank Hill (see above), is probably a late sixteenth century invention, although it is quite likely that it was called Brough by the local Old English-speaking population after the departure of the Romans.

Conisbrough still has its medieval stone castle, which is discussed below, and Mexborough still has the remains of an early Norman motte and bailey castle, but to what features the Anglo-Saxons were referring when they gave their burgh names to the places listed above is still open to speculation. It is possible that they were referring to Iron Age, Roman or Romano-British fortifications that were already deserted when they arrived or which they had overcome as their settlement spread westwards up the Don and Dearne valleys. The burgh in Burghwallis, for example, may refer to the minor Roman fort near Robin Hood's Well on the A1 less than a kilometre west of the village.

MOTTE AND BAILEY CASTLES

South Yorkshire contains the sites of thirteen 'motte and bailey' castles dating from the early Norman period. They were erected by local Norman lords in the years immediately following the Norman Conquest in 1066 and during the civil wars in the reign of King Stephen (1135-54). They consist of a motte, which was a steeply sloping mound, partly or wholly artificial, on which there would be a timber tower, surrounded by a courtyard with outbuildings (the bailey), which in turn was surrounded by a ditch. Entrance to the bailey was usually over a timber bridge which spanned the ditch. Seven of the known sites are in a good state of preservation, and can be visited or, if on private property, can be easily seen from neighbouring vantage points. The one at Bradfield, which can be viewed from the churchyard, has a motte nearly 20 metres high; at Kimberworth only the motte survives, surrounded by housing; at Mexborough the castle is part of a park, and, both motte and bailey and surrounding ditch are impressive and in a good state of preservation; so is the one at Laughton which can be viewed from the churchyard; at Langthwaite off the A638 to the south of Adwick le Street, both motte and bailey have survived, encircled by a very wide ditch; and finally at Thorne, the motte survives in a public park north of the church. Plans and photographs of some of these motte and bailey castles are shown in Figure 7.5.

STONE KEEP AND BAILEY CASTLES

South Yorkshire had three magnificent castles with stone keeps in the medieval period at Sheffield, Tickhill and Conisbrough, built by powerful Norman lords who owned extensive estates. All that remains of the one at Sheffield are lower parts of walls preserved below the Castle Market. It was built in the second half of the thirteenth century after the existing motte and bailey castle, at the confluence of the Don and its tributary the Sheaf where the two rivers provided natural moats on the north and east, had been destroyed by fire. It was demolished at the end of the 1640s after the Civil War and precise details of its plan have not survived, although excavations carried out in the 1920s revealed stretches of stone wall, a circular bastion next to the main gateway, and possibly part of the gatehouse and its drawbridge support. Earlier in the century, Thomas

(a)(i)

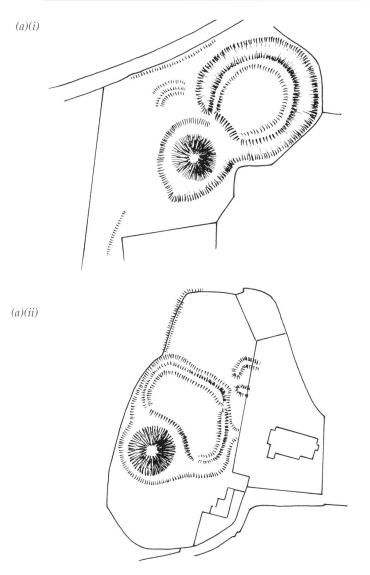

(a)(ii)

(b)(i)

(b)(ii)

Figure 7.5. *Motte and bailey castles: (a) Plans: (i) Mexborough and (ii) Laughton en le Morthen. (b) Photographs: (i) Mexborough and (ii) Thorne.* Photographs by the Author.

Winder, who worked for many years in the Duke of Norfolk's estate office in Sheffield, put together a rough sketch map of the castle site based on old maps he had consulted and this is shown in Figure 7.6. On Winder's sketch map, the moat on the west and south of Castle Hill demarcates the inner bailey within which the keep stood. It has been suggested that an outer bailey ran south from the moat up the slope as far as the modern Fitzalan Square.

Sheffield Castle attained national significance as the main prison for Mary Queen of Scots between 1570-84. By that time the castle and the manor of Sheffield had descended to George, sixth Earl of Shrewsbury, and one of the reasons why Queen Elizabeth chose him to be Mary's jailer, was his ownership of a number of well fortified castles and houses, including Sheffield, which were also away from major highways. Outwardly forbidding and probably draughty, Sheffield Castle in Elizabethan times was not without its comforts. An inventory of the castle and the nearby Manor Lodge of 1582 listed a large number of wall hangings including 'Forrest worke', 'ye storye of Hercules' and the 'storye of the Passion'. There were also various chimney hangings and more than a score of 'Turkey carpetts'. The window curtains were of taffeta, silk, satin and buckram, and the coverings , curtains and counterpanes of the tester beds were of crimson and purple velvet, satin, and silk embroidered with silver and gold.

Although the keep has gone (again at the end of the 1640s after the Civil War), much more of Tickhill Castle (Figure 7.7) has survived than of its counterpart in Sheffield, although it is now private property and can only be viewed from the outside. Like Sheffield, the first castle at Tickhill was a motte and bailey castle dominated by a motte which was 23 metres high and 25 metres in diameter. The bottom third of the motte was probably a natural hill called Tica's hill which gave rise to the name Tickhill. The rest of the motte was built up by

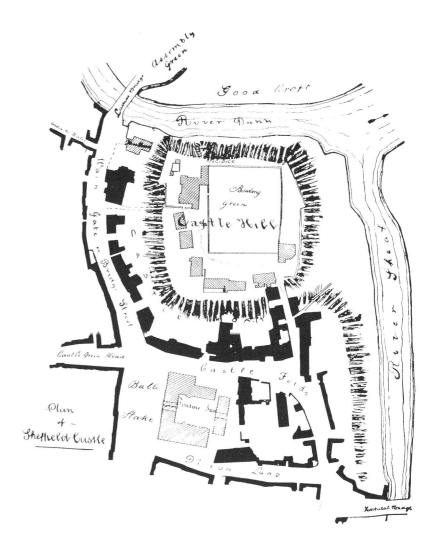

Figure 7.6. *Thomas Winder's sketch map of the site of Sheffield Castle.*

Norman castle builders and an army of labourers. The motte and bailey castle was constructed in the late eleventh century by Roger de Busli as the centre of authority for his extensive estate in South Yorkshire, and neighbouring Nottinghamshire, Derbyshire, Lincolnshire and Leicestershire, collectively called the Honour of Tickhill. The timber buildings and rampart of the motte and bailey castle were destroyed in 1102, when de Busli's successor backed a failed pretender to the English throne and the castle at Tickhill became the property of the Crown. Over the course of the next century Tickhill Castle was transformed into a stone castle with a stone curtain wall surrounding the bailey and a massive gatehouse (erected 1129-

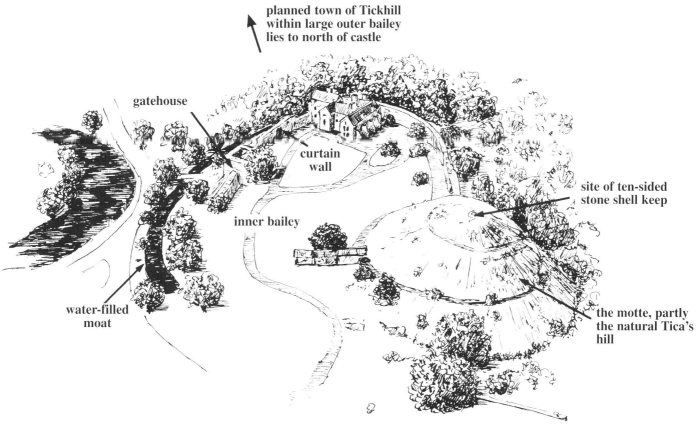

Figure 7.7. *Tickhill Castle: aerial view from the south showing the site of the keep, the curtain wall of the inner bailey, the gatehouse, and the moat partly hidden in the trees.*

30). A water-filled moat, which still survives in the west and south, surrounded the walled bailey. A ten-sided cylindrical stone keep was erected on the motte about 50 years later. The keep at Tickhill appears to have been a 'shell keep', especially adapted to sit on an artificial motte which might not be able to support the weight of a large, tall keep. In this type of keep the outer walls simply provided an elevated defensive wall for an internal courtyard which was not roofed over. Buildings were built against the inner wall of the shell. The surviving walled bailey at Tickhill is in fact an inner bailey; extending northwards was an outer bailey protected by an earthwork. Within the outer bailey the planned town of Tickhill was laid out. This is considered in greater detail in Chapter 12.

The outstanding stone castle in South Yorkshire is, of course, Conisbrough Castle, standing aloft on a tiny 'island' of Magnesian Limestone and controlling an important crossing-point on the River Don (Figure 7.8). To quote the official guidebook, the keep is ' one of the finest surviving pieces of twelfth-century secular architecture in the country'. Like Sheffield and Tickhill, Conisbrough Castle began life as a motte and bailey castle in the years immediately after the Norman Conquest of 1066, under the aegis of William de Warenne who had fought beside King William at Hastings. Subsequently, he had been granted large and scattered estates by the Conqueror. But de Warenne was not the first to establish a fortification at Conisbrough: the name, which it is assumed

Figure 7.8. Conisbrough Castle: (a) plan of barbican, inner bailey and keep); (b) view of the curtain wall and buttressed keep from the inner bailey, with ruins of the hall and kitchen in the foreground. Photograph by the Author.

(a)

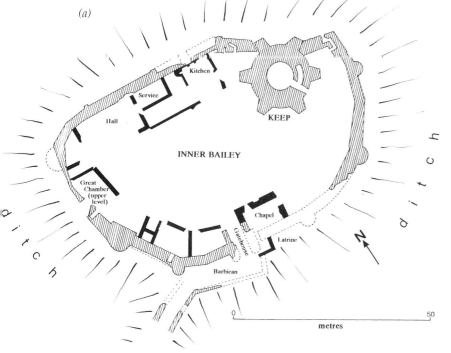

(b)

pre-dates the coming of the Normans, is partly Old Norse and partly Old English, and means 'king's stronghold', but to which king the name refers is unknown. The stone castle dates from the last two decades of the twelfth century and was built under the direction of Hamelin Plantagenet, the illegitimate half-brother of Henry II, who was the second husband of the third earl of Warenne's only surviving offspring, Isobel.

The visitor today is only aware of the walled inner bailey and the keep, but originally there was an outer bailey to the west. The inner bailey is protected by a massive curtain wall at the top of a natural hill of Magnesian Limestone whose slopes have been artificially steepened. The curtain wall is mostly of rubble (angular, undressed stone) and the south side was originally reinforced by six projecting turrets, three of which survive. The curtain wall is splayed out at the bottom to give added stability and to cause objects thrown from the top of the wall to ricochet outwards at attackers.

The inner bailey gatehouse is approached via a narrow walled causeway over the wide, deep ditch. This is called a barbican and was overlooked from the curtain wall. Its function was to give added protection to the gate - the weakest point in the castle's defences. Important domestic buildings, built largely of timber including a hall, a kitchen and a chapel, were built against the inner face of the curtain wall. Little remains of these buildings. On either side of the keep are garderobes (privies) built into the curtain wall.

Dominating all is the stone keep, a massive cylindrical tower, nearly 30 metres high and with walls more than 4.6 metres thick. Unlike the rubble curtain wall, the keep is constructed of dressed limestone blocks (called ashlar blocks). Attached to the basic cylinder shape are six splayed buttresses which rise to become turrets above the roof line. The keep is entered at first floor level into what was probably a store room. Steps lead down to a ground floor room which contains a well: the keep

had its own water supply. At second-floor level is the lord's great chamber and above that, on the third floor is his bedchamber and chapel. A staircase from the third floor leads to a parapet at the top of the keep. Rising above this are the buttress-turrets, four of which are hollow: two originally contained water cisterns, another an oven, and the fourth appears to have been a pigeon loft (an emergency food supply?!).

Conisbrough Castle was in disrepair by Elizabethan times and was never garrisoned during the Civil War in the 1640s. This saved it from the destruction (called 'slighting') that befell both Sheffield and Tickhill. Now the floors of the keep have been reinstated and the conical roof is once more in place.

FORTIFIED HOUSES

There are about thirty moated house sites in South Yorkshire and many more have doubtless been filled in and built over. Dodsworth, the seventeenth century antiquary, for example, recorded that before it had been pulled down, Cowley Manor at Chapeltown had been 'a stately castle-like house moated about', and at nearby Thorpe Hesley, John Harrison in his survey of the Manor of Sheffield described Hesley Hall as 'moated round'. Neither of these moats now exist.

Moated sites probably all belong to the late thirteenth and early fourteenth centuries. The one at Tankersley (Figure 7.9a) probably surrounded the medieval manor house before it was re-built in the deer park in the sixteenth century. The Hangthwaite moat (Figure 7.9b) was most likely the successor to the motte and bailey castle which lies 250 metres to the west.

Parts of one of the most unusual fortifications around a house in South Yorkshire survive at Houndhill, near Barnsley. These were built by Richard Elmhirst, an ardent Royalist, in the Civil War of 1642-49 in the form of stone walls and turreted watch towers. One of the turrets survives.

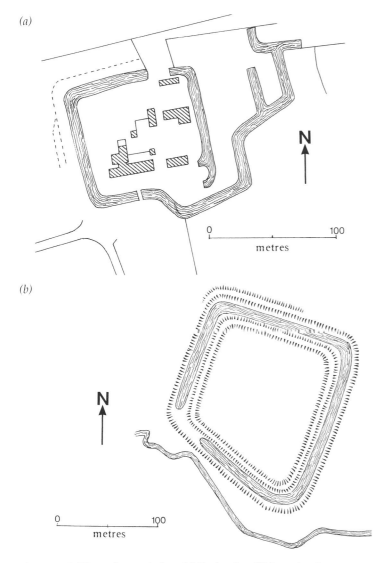

(a)

(b)

Figure 7. 9. Plans of moated sites: (a) Tankersley; (b) Langthwaite.

What to read about South Yorkshire's forts and castles

ELLIOTT, BRIAN, (1999) *Discovering South Yorkshire,* Smith Settle.
HEY, DAVID (1979) *The Making of South Yorkshire,* Moorland Publishing, Chapters 1 and 7.
JONES, MELVYN (1990) *Wincobank Hill: Heritage Site and Vantage Point,* interpretive leaflet, Sheffield City Council, Department of Land & Planning.
PEVSNER, SIR N. (1959) *The Buildings of England: Yorkshire, The West Riding,* Penguin Books.
RYDER, PETER (1982) *Medieval Buildings of Yorkshire,* Ash Grove Books.

Places to visit

The Iron Age forts on **Wincobank Hill** and in **Scholes Coppice** can be visited at any time.
There is free access at all times to **Carl Wark** fort in the Burbage valley (grid reference SK 259815).
The best places to see the **Roman Ridge** are near Little Common Lane at Kimberworth, on Barber Balk Road on the Kimberworth Park housing estate, and in Wath Wood.
The **Bar Dyke** can be seen 2¹/₂ kilometres north-west of High Bradfield on either side of the road to Midhopestones.
Doncaster Museum has good displays about Roman Doncaster.
Weston Park Museum, Sheffield, has displays on **Sheffield Castle** and **Templeborough Roman fort.**
The pillars from the granary at Templeborough Roman fort can be seen in the gardens at **Clifton Park Museum,** Rotherham.
The motte and bailey castles at **Bradfield** and **Laughton en le Morthen** can both be seen from neighbouring churchyards. The motte and bailey castles at **Mexborough** (in Castle Hill Grounds) and **Thorne** are in areas open to the public at all times.
Conisbrough Castle is in the guardianship of English Heritage and is open all the year round.

BUILDING IN TIMBER AND STONE

SO NATURALLY do the traditional buildings of South Yorkshire, constructed of Millstone Grit and Coal Measure sandstones in the west and central zones and Magnesian Limestone and brick and tile in the east, sit in the landscape, that it is difficult to imagine that for all but military and religious structures, building in stone and brick is a post-medieval characteristic. Cottages, farmhouses and other farm buildings, the vast majority of the houses of the gentry, and most of the buildings in the towns were wholly or half timbered in the medieval period. The massive twelfth and thirteenth century castles at Sheffield, Conisbrough and Tickhill, and the great monastic houses of Roche and Monk Bretton, and the smaller ones at Beauchief and Ecclesfield were of stone. So were the parish churches, including the splendid Perpendicular re-buildings at places such as Ecclesfield, Rotherham and Tickhill. But domestic building in stone or brick was rare. As late as about 1540 John Leland, the antiquary, on his six-year tour of England, described Doncaster as 'buildid of wodde, and the houses be slatid: yet is there great plenty of stone there about.'

BUILDING IN TIMBER

In South Yorkshire's surviving timber framed buildings trees from the county's medieval woods can be seen. I say trees because in the Middle Ages the carpenter did not buy his timber in the form of ready sawn and shaped planks and beams, he selected trees in woods and hedges that would roughly square up to the dimensions of the components required with the minimum of shaping. For great beams a large tree of 60-75 years of age with a diameter of 15-18 inches would be chosen, and for rafters much younger trees about eight inches in diameter would be felled.

The timber used was almost always oak and it was sawn or shaped with an axe or adze while it was still 'green', for ease of working, as shown in the celebrated scenes from the Bayeux Tapestry. Carpentry techniques were developed to capitalise on the natural shapes and properties of the trees.

There were two complementary traditions of timber framed building in medieval South Yorkshire: **post** and **truss structures** and **cruck buildings.**

Post and truss structures

A post and truss building (Figure 8.1) consisted of a series of trusses or cross frames formed by a pair of vertical posts (principal posts) standing on large stones (stylobates) and connected by tie beams. Longitudinally, the tops of the

Figure 8.1. Constructional features of a post and truss building.

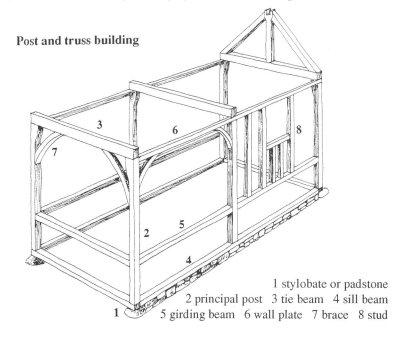

Post and truss building

1 stylobate or padstone
2 principal post   3 tie beam   4 sill beam
5 girding beam   6 wall plate   7 brace   8 stud

principal posts were connected by horizontal timbers, called wall plates (connecting the tops of the posts), girding beams (at mid-wall level) and sill beams (at or near ground level). For extra stability curved braces were used between principal post and wall plate, principal post and girding beam, and between principal post and tie beam. The walls were framed by vertical timbers called studs, with the spaces between filled with wattle and daub, stone slates covered with plaster or horizontal split oak laths, again covered by plaster. The roofs were of the common rafter type or the principal rafter type. The rafters in common rafter roofs were strengthened by collars just below the apex; in principal rafter roofs in South Yorkshire, the principal rafters were supported by a vertical post rising from the tie beam, called a king post. Surviving post and truss buildings of medieval or immediate post-medieval age include the thirteenth century Whiston Manorial Barn, Nether Fold farmhouse, Thorpe Hesley (timber felled c.1495), the Old Queen's Head, Sheffield (timbers felled c.1506-

Figure 8.2. Interior of Whiston Manorial Barn.

1510), Bishops' House, Sheffield (c. 1525) and Gunthwaite Hall Barn (sixteenth century?).

Whiston Manorial Barn is probably of thirteenth century date. It originally consisted of five bays (a bay is the space between two trusses), but in the sixteenth century the building was extended by two more bays and the original timber walls were replaced by stone. Figure 8.2 shows the interior looking west. On the left is a principal post with two braces to the wall plate and one to the tie beam. Whiston Manorial Barn is an example of an aisled post and truss building. In this type of building extra building width was achieved by erecting the long walls beyond the principal posts to which they were connected by extensions to the roof trusses. Aisle ties (short sections of timber connecting the principal posts with the tops of the long walls) and wind braces (curved pieces of timber connecting the principal posts to the long walls) were added to strengthen the overall structure. In Figure 8.2 the principal post in the centre has both an aisle tie and a wind brace.

Bishops' House is an L-shaped yeoman's house built c. 1500-1550 (Figure 8.3). It is now a museum and open to the public. The original house (the east wing and the southern part of the west wing) was completely framed in timber, but the timber framing on the ground floor has been largely replaced by stone, and a northern extension to the west wing was built in stone in the seventeenth century. The timber framed house has a king post roof originally supported on a frame of vertical and horizontal oak timbers tied together with mortise and tenon joints and wooden pegs (treenails). Except for the corner principal posts, the timber framing at ground floor level has been replaced by stone. As a protection against damp the principal posts all originally stood on large stones (stylobates or padstones), some of which can still be seen, and the lowest horizontal timbers (the sill beams) rested on low stone walls.

As Figure 8.3 shows, a variety of patterns of timberwork was employed on the external walls with herring-bone patterns employed on both wings. What is very noticeable everywhere on the building is that the timbers (studs) are closely spaced, with the spaces between them not much wider than the studs themselves. This close studding is a typical feature of timber framed buildings in the north of England. In the spaces between the studs split oak laths were fixed horizontally into grooves cut into the sides of the studs and then covered with plaster.

Inside the house, there are carpenter's marks on the first floor wall of the west wing, adze marks on the shaped timber beside the stair head, thick oak planks used to make the floors when upper rooms were put in the east wing in the seventeenth century, and elaborately carved oak panelling of seventeenth century date in the hall on the ground floor of the east wing.

Cruck buildings

In a cruck building (Figure 8.4) the weight is carried on pairs of timbers called cruck blades which rise from or near the ground and meet at the apex of the roof. The blades are usually curved, having been selected from naturally bent trees. Often a curved trunk was split or sawn lengthways to make two matching blades. The structure is normally strengthened by tie beams connecting each pair of blades. If it was not convenient to have tie beams across the interior of the building, the wall plates were carried on spurs projecting from the back of the cruck blade and supported on a short vertical post. The roof of a cruck building was stabilised by struts called windbraces. When such buildings had timber walls, the ends of the tie beams carried longitudinal wall plates. In the timber walls vertical studs rose from sill beams to the wall plates. The gaps

Figure 8.4. Constructional features of a cruck framed building.

Cruck framing

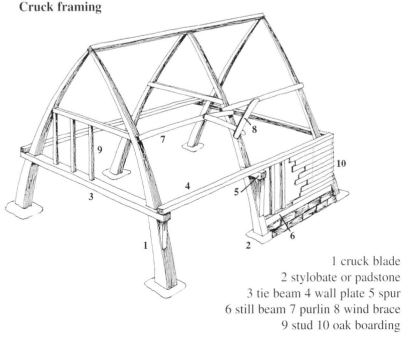

1 cruck blade
2 stylobate or padstone
3 tie beam 4 wall plate 5 spur
6 still beam 7 purlin 8 wind brace
9 stud 10 oak boarding

Figure 8.3. Bishops' House, Sheffield. Joan Jones

between the studs were filled by a variety of materials as in post and truss structures or, alternatively, the entire wall could be covered by horizontal oak boarding. One of the best surviving cruck buildings is Oaks Fold Barn in Concord Park, Sheffield. (Figure 8.5). Other cruck buildings, often encased in stone, have survived unrecorded until relatively recently, such as the building housing Court House Antiques in Ecclesfield.

It is interesting to note that although post and truss structures are found throughout South Yorkshire, only a handful of the known cruck buildings (about 150 surviving cruck structures and others demolished since 1900 have been recorded) are outside the western half of the county. In South Yorkshire cruck construction was a Pennine and Pennine fringe tradition. There are also relatively few surviving or 'lost' medieval timber framed buildings in the Magnesian Limestone belt - a zone where timber resources were scarce because settlement had taken place there early and a very large

Figure 8.5. Interior of Oaks Fold Barn, Concord Park, Sheffield. The Author

proportion of the woodland had been cleared by the time of the Domesday survey in 1086.

Before leaving the use of timber in buildings it is also worth noting that timber and wood were the raw materials for the important craft of wood carving for decoration. The best surviving examples in South Yorkshire are in churches, such as the early fourteenth century knight at Barnburgh, the fifteenth century nave roof in Rotherham parish church and the fifteenth century carved bench ends in the chancel at Ecclesfield (especially the madonna and child and St Katherine with her wheel). There are also some particularly fine carvings on the exterior of the Old Queen's Head public house in Sheffield (formerly a hunting lodge and banqueting house in the deer park).

BUILDING IN STONE

South Yorkshire is particularly well endowed with workable building stone. In the west the Millstone Grit outcrops were worked for their hard, pale sandstones which were particularly resistant to weathering; the Coal Measure sandstones are softer but more workable, with a wide range of colouring from a soft yellow to the rich red of the Mexborough ('Rotherham Red') Rock; the Magnesian Limestone quarries yielded a creamy, friable stone. Where stone was not locally available it was transported from neighbouring or more distant parishes.

There is a long local tradition of building in rubble and ashlar blocks. Rubble work is angular pieces of rock either laid in courses or uncoursed (Figure 8.6 (a)) or, more rarely, in a herring-bone pattern (Figure 8.6 (b)). Ashlar blocks are carefully worked square, oblong or curved blocks of stone laid in courses (Figure 8.6 (c)). They were only used in high status buildings in the middle ages but by the late eighteenth and nineteenth centuries even small cottages (especially

(a)

(c)

Figure 8.6. *(a) Rubble work in the curtain wall of the inner bailey at Conisbrough Castle. (b) Saxon herring-bone work at St Helen's parish church at Burghwallis. (c) Ashlar blocks in the keep at Conisbrough Castle. (d) Pebbles, the major constituents in the walls of the nave and clerestory at St Nicholas' parish church, Thorne.* The Author

(b)

(d)

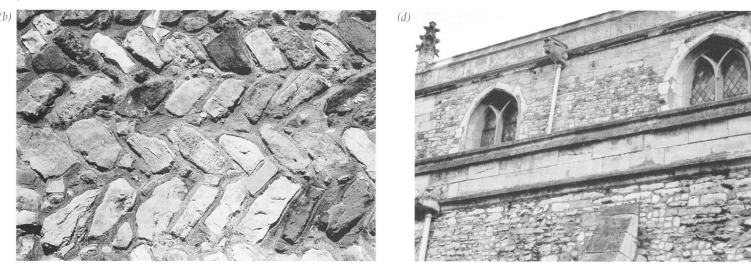

gatehouses at the entrances to large country parks as at Wentworth, Wortley and Sandbeck) were sometimes built of finely dressed stone. In the western half of the county dressed gritstone or hard sandstone were used for quoin work (stones laid alternately 'long and short' at the corners of buildings), for window lintels and sills, and for door jambs and lintels. Thinly split sandstone eventually replaced thatch as the favoured roof covering in the western and central parts of the county, being replaced by pantiles in the Magnesian Limestone belt and in the lowlands to the east. In Figure 8.7 the use of stone at Kirkstead Abbey Grange, a fifteenth or sixteenth century house in which materials from earlier buildings were extensively re-used, is illustrated.

In the eastern lowlands, building stone for vernacular buildings was scarce or involved the cost of transporting it from the west or up river from the coast, and brick and pantiles, rather than stone, became the common building materials after the decline in the use of timber. Pebbles, of water-borne and glacial origin, were sometimes incorporated into early stone buildings (Figure 8.6 (d)).

Local stone was extensively used in the building of the larger houses of the gentry and aristocracy from the sixteenth to the nineteenth century (Figure 8.8). Two particularly interesting sixteenth century survivals, although one is a ruin, are the Turret House at Sheffield Manor Lodge and the facade at Thorpe Salvin Hall. The Turret House at Sheffield Manor Lodge was built by the sixth Earl of Shrewsbury roughly between 1574-1583 as an addition to the existing Lodge, at a high point in his 2,500 acre deer park. It is reputed to have been a prison of Mary Queen of Scots, but, although she was imprisoned at the Lodge at various times, the size and location of the Turret House makes the suggestion implausible. The Turret House, is three storeys high and is built of local sandstone in coursed rubble with massive sandstone quoins.

Thorpe Salvin Hall (Figure 8.8 (a)) is an impressive ruin with only the south facade and gatehouse surviving. It was abandoned in the 1690s when the then owner, the Duke of Leeds, moved into the newly-built Kiveton Park (built in brick with limestone decorative work, but demolished in 1811). Built in local limestone, the three-storey south front at Thorpe Salvin consists of two corner towers, two massive chimney stacks and a central porch, separated by three walls pierced by mullioned and transomed windows. The gatehouse has a square doorway with a heavy lintel and its steep gable end is stepped.

Mid- and late seventeenth century houses of note are Bullhouse Hall near Penistone, Kimberworth Manor House, Hellaby Hall and Cannon Hall at Cawthorne. Bullhouse Hall is a mid-seventeenth century manor house built for the Puritan Sylvanus Rich. It is an atmospheric building constructed of

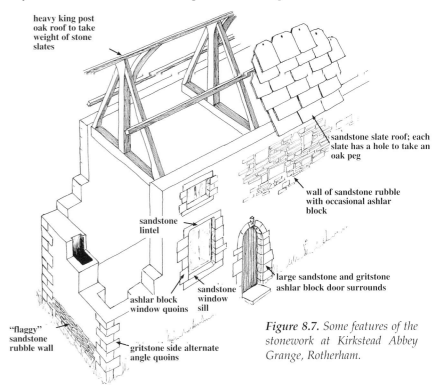

heavy king post oak roof to take weight of stone slates

sandstone slate roof; each slate has a hole to take an oak peg

wall of sandstone rubble with occasional ashlar block

sandstone lintel

large sandstone and gritstone ashlar block door surrounds

ashlar block window quoins

sandstone window sill

"flaggy" sandstone rubble wall

gritstone side alternate angle quoins

Figure 8.7. Some features of the stonework at Kirkstead Abbey Grange, Rotherham.

(a)

(b)

Figure 8.8. *(a) Thorpe Salvin Hall and gatehouse. (b) Kimberworth Manor House. (c) Thundercliffe Grange. (d) Brodsworth Hall.* Photographs by The Author

(c)

(d)

sandstone ashlar blocks with a series of steep gables and mullioned windows. Kimberworth Manor House (Figure 8.8 (b)), built for the Kent family about 1694, is also a house of steep gables which contain oval windows. The walls are of pale sandstone but the quoins, window surrounds and string courses are in the distinctive Rotherham Red sandstone. Hellaby Hall, now a hotel, was built at the end of the seventeenth century for Ralph Fretwell, a successful Barbados sugar planter, and has a distinct Dutch look about it. This arises from the unusual design of the gable (which rises from large spirals by a series of slopes and curves to a flat apex), and the use of pantiles on the roof. The walls are of local Magnesian Limestone, with the front faced in finely dressed ashlar limestone blocks from quarries at Roche. Finally, Cannon Hall was built for the Spencer family, leading members of the syndicate that almost monopolised the charcoal iron industry in South Yorkshire and North Derbyshire. Of the present house, the central five blocks, two and a half storeys high and topped by a balustrade, is of late seventeenth century date.

The eighteenth century saw the building of a substantial number of country houses in local stone including Wentworth Castle, Wentworth Woodhouse (twice), Wortley, Cusworth, Sandbeck Park and Thundercliffe Grange. At Wentworth Castle (formerly Stainborough Hall) an enlargement in the Baroque style was built between about 1709-14 by Thomas Wentworth, who had aspired to the Wentworth Woodhouse estate on the death of the Earl of Strafford in 1695, but was not mentioned in his will and succeeded only to the baronetcy and a minor title. He then bought Stainborough Hall from the indebted Cutler family and proceeded to try to out-build his rival at Wentworth Woodhouse. Baroque is a term used for the architectural style used in English country houses between 1685-1715. It was based on the classical architecture of Greece and Rome, and was sometimes florid. The Baroque (east) range at Wentworth Castle is fifteen bays wide and two and a half storeys high, with a rich display of leaves and fruit above the three central first floor windows. The first floor is one long gallery 55 metres long. Sir Nicholas Pevsner called the building 'a showpiece of almost megalomaniac magnificence'. A Baroque house was started at Wentworth Woodhouse facing west by the 1st Marquis of Rockingham in 1724 but before it was quite finished and furnished he began to build a much larger house facing east in the Palladian style. The two houses are joined together back-to-back but it is the Palladian mansion that can be seen by the public from Wentworth park (see Figure 10.5). The Palladian style is a much more restrained classical style than the Baroque, based on the work of the renaissance architect Andrea Palladio. At Wentworth Woodhouse the east Palladian front is 183 metres long, the longest country house front in England. When the first Marquis died in 1750, the house was still unfinished. It had by then cost £90,000, many millions of pounds in today's money. There was, of course a response from Wentworth Castle, a Palladian south range was built between 1760 and 1765.

Cusworth Hall, Wentworth Castle, Wortley Hall and Thundercliffe Grange (Figure 8.8 (c)) have in common the fact that either John Platt senior (1700-1743) or his son John Platt junior (1728-1810), the Rotherham-based mason-architects, were closely involved in their construction. John Platt senior was involved in the design and building of the Palladian north front at Cusworth Hall in 1741. His son was employed on various commissions at Wortley Hall and he seems to have been solely responsible for building Thundercliffe Grange for the Earl of Effingham between 1776 and 1783. On the Palladian front at Wentworth Castle John Platt junior was responsible for the six Corinthian capitals, the carved pediment and probably the finer masonry.

The gem of nineteenth century country house building in local stone is Brodsworth Hall, opened to the public in 1995. The house was built in the Italianate style in 1861-62 for Charles Sabine Thellusson, with some of the stone (Magnesian Limestone) being quarried in the grounds. Quarries are visible in the gardens. The soft Magnesian Limestone used at Brodsworth suffered badly from weathering and by 1990 when it was acquired by English Heritage, parts of the walls were riddled with holes in which birds were nesting. Substantial restoration work has taken place and it now looks much as it must have done immediately after its completion (Figure 8.8 (d)).

Stone-built churches and abbeys are discussed in the next chapter.

Places to visit

The following buildings are open to the public: **Bishops' House**, Sheffield (museum); **Brodsworth Hall** (English Heritage); **Cannon Hall** (museum); **Court House Antiques** (antiques centre with coffee shop); **Cusworth Hall** (museum); **Hellaby Hall** (hotel); **Old Queen's Head** (public house); **St Mary's parish church**, Ecclesfield (1.30-2.30p.m., Mondays to Fridays); **Wentworth Castle** (college).

The interiors of **Barnburgh parish church** and **Oaks Fold Barn** can be viewed by appointment.

Whiston Manorial Barn and **Wortley Hall** are both open for public events periodically.

Thorpe Salvin Hall and gateway can be viewed from the roadside and the Palladian range at **Wentworth Woodhouse** can be viewed from public footpaths in Wentworth Park.

Laughton en le Morthen is an interesting village to visit to see the use of Rotherham Red Sandstone and Magnesian Limestone in the walls of buildings and Coal Measure sandstone slates and pantiles in roofs. The parish church, Old Hall Farm and the early seventeenth century school are worth a close inspection.

What to read about timber and stone buildings

BEASTALL, T. W. (1995) 'Sandbeck Hall and Park' in M. Jones (ed.) *Aspects of Rotherham 1*, Wharncliffe Publishing, pp. 89-98.

ELLIOTT, B (1998) 'Architects of no slender merit: Platt of Rotherham, 1700-1810' in M. Jones (ed.) *Aspects of Rotherham 3*, Wharncliffe Publishing, pp. 113-133.

HARRIS, R. (1979) *Discovering Timber-Framed Buildings*, second edition, Shire Publications Ltd.

HEY, D (1979) *The Making of South Yorkshire*, Moorland Publishing.

HEY, D. (1981) *Buildings of Britain, 1550-1750: Yorkshire*, Moorland Publishing.

JONES, M (1993) *Sheffield's Woodland Heritage*. second edition, Green Tree Publications.

JONES, M. (1995) 'Rents, Remarks and Observations: the first Marquis of Rockingham's Rent Roll Book' in M. Jones (ed.) *Aspects of Rotherham 1*, Wharncliffe Publishing, pp. 113-128.

PEVSNER, SIR N. (1959) *The Buildings of England, Yorkshire: The West Riding*, Penguin Books.

RYDER, P. (1979) *Timber Framed Buildings in South Yorkshire*, South Yorkshire County Council.

RYDER, P. (1982) *Medieval Buildings of Yorkshire*, Ash Grove Books.

SMITH, P. G. (1997) 'Charles Sabine Augustus Thellusson and Italianate buildings on the Brodsworth estate' in B. Elliott (ed.) *Aspects of Doncaster 1*, Wharncliffe Publishing, pp. 75-86.

THE CHURCH IN THE LANDSCAPE

THIS CHAPTER EXAMINES the impact of religious institutions on the landscape of South Yorkshire. Not just parish churches, but also church territories (parishes), accommodation for the clergy, church schools, nonconformist chapels, and monasteries and nunneries and their estates.

MEDIEVAL PARISHES

The first churches and the first priests in South Yorkshire were responsible for much larger areas than churches today. Christianity had reached South Yorkshire before the arrival of the Anglo-Saxons in the seventh century as revealed by the Anglo-Saxon place-names Ecclesfield and Ecclesall, the *eccles* element, as already pointed out, being the Anglo-Saxon name for a pre-existing Celtic Christian church. By the time of the Domesday survey fifteen places were recorded with churches but this number is an underestimate - the church at Laughton en le Morthen, for example, incorporates an Anglo-Saxon doorway but is not mentioned in the Domesday Book.

The first churches were called minster churches (from the word monastery) and their territories were very large. They were the 'mother churches' from which the gospel was preached in their hinterlands. In South Yorkshire it is believed that churches at Ecclesfield, Silkstone and Conisbrough fulfilled this function in the late Saxon period. Ecclesfield was still referred to as the 'Mynster of the Moores' in the seventeenth century, and the nave at St. Peter's Church at Conisbrough is an

Anglo-Saxon structure. No pre-Conquest structure remains at Silkstone. Where no pre-Conquest structures survive there are often Anglo-Saxon crosses surviving in churchyards or built into the fabric of later stone churches as at Cawthorne, Thrybergh, High Melton and Sprotbrough, for example. The magnificent tenth century Sheffield cross is in the British Museum but a replica can be seen in Weston Park Museum. All these crosses may have been preaching crosses.

By 1200 most places had a church - probably still in timber in many cases - built usually by the local lord of the manor, although some churches were 'multi-manorial', built at the expense of a number of landowners. Because the priest's living was based on a tenth (a tithe) of all the produce of the lord and his tenants, there emerged a pattern of churches with surrounding parishes, the parish providing both the tithe and the congregation. Figure 9.1 shows, in simplified form, the

Figure 9.1. Ecclesiastical parishes in medieval South Yorkshire. For an explanation of the letters A - I see the text.

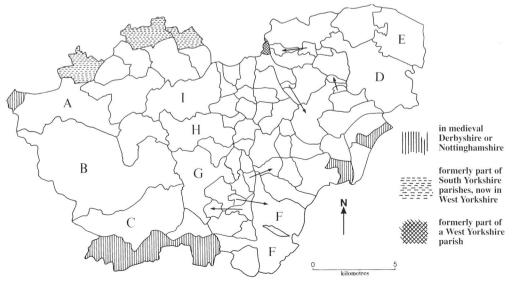

in medieval
**Derbyshire or
Nottinghamshire**

formerly part of
**South Yorkshire
parishes, now in
West Yorkshire**

formerly part of
**a West Yorkshire
parish**

parish map of South Yorkshire at the end of the medieval period. The pattern broadly reflects the density of population which in turn reflects the varying physical conditions in which the majority of the population was subsisting through farming the land. The biggest parishes were in the west on the Millstone Grit and western half of the Coal Measures (Penistone (A), Ecclesfield (B) and Sheffield (C)), and in the north-east on the Humberhead Levels (e.g., Hatfield (D) which until 1326 included Thorne (E)). In both areas, for different environmental reasons, village settlement was much less common than in the rest of the county and populations were smaller and more dispersed. By contrast, in the eastern part of the Coal Measures and in the Magnesian Limestone belt, where population was relatively dense, settlement was overwhelmingly nucleated in villages, and parishes were small, except in the case of Laughton en le Morthen (F) which was as large as the parishes further west on the Lower and Middle Coal Measures, and like them contained a number of subsidiary villages, hamlets and farms.

Medieval churches occupy a variety of sites. In the small central parishes they were generally built in the centre of the main and usually the only settlement in the parish. Further west where the parishes were increasingly larger and their long axis often ran east-west, the medieval parish churches are mostly located in the east in the middle of the richest farming land and/or at an important transport node, such as a bridging point, in the village that gave the parish its name - as at Rotherham (G), Wath (H), Darfield (I), Penistone (A), Ecclesfield (B) and Sheffield (C). Covering more than 20,000 hectares or 78 square miles, Ecclesfield was the largest parish in South Yorkshire and the western two-thirds was, except in name, a separate parish from as early as the mid-twelfth century and a church was built near the motte and bailey castle in the hamlet of High Bradfield which was referred to as 'Kirk Town'. Where

available, churches were sometimes sited on a commanding eminence as at Penistone, Ecclesfield, Rotherham, Whiston and Laughton en le Morthen. They were also located near to manorial halls or castles as at Bradfield, Hickleton, Laughton en le Morthen and Thorne. There are also well-known examples in other parts of the country of churches sited near earlier pagan shrines, but there is only one possible example of this practice in South Yorkshire, at Throapham, between Laughton and Dinnington, where St John's church is located well outside the hamlet on the presumed site of a holy well.

MEDIEVAL CHURCHES

Medieval churches are aligned, as far as is possible, east-west, often set in a churchyard that is much more extensive on the south than the north because it was believed the north side was the Devil's side. The church itself is made up of three basic elements: nave, chancel and tower, and the rest is elaboration. These elements can be arranged in two ways. In the most common plan the tower is at the west end, then comes the nave (from the Latin word for ship) for the congregation, and at the east end, the chancel, for the clergy, originally separated from the nave by the chancel arch. Less commonly the tower is located above the joining of the nave and chancel, and there are north and south extensions (transepts) at this point, making a cross-like (cruciform) plan. These basic plans were extended by the building of aisles to the north and south of the nave, side chapels, most commonly constructed out of the aisles at the chancel end, and porches. The earliest timber churches were replaced by churches built in local sandstone or limestone. Only in the eastern lowlands, where stone had to be 'imported', did church builders have to resort to materials other than quarried stone. Pebbles were used in the earliest stone churches at Fishlake and Hatfield, and the entire early thirteenth century walls of the nave (including the clerestory)

(a)

(c)

Figure 9.2. *Examples of Anglo-Saxon, Norman and Gothic church building in South Yorkshire: (a) Anglo-Saxon doorway at All Saints', Laughton en le Morthen; (b) Norman doorway at St. Cuthbert's, Fishlake; (c) Perpendicular church, St Mary's, Tickhill; (d) Perpendicular church, All Saints', Rotherham.* The Author

(b)

(d)

and twelfth century bottom stage of the tower at St Nicholas' church at Thorne are constructed mainly of pebbles. Pebbles were also heavily used in the construction of St Oswald's parish church at Kirk Sandall.

Churches were rebuilt and parts re-modelled throughout the medieval period and there was much alteration of medieval churches in the Victorian period. But much evidence of early church building remains. There are four widely recognised churches of Saxon date in South Yorkshire. The nave at St Peter's church at Conisbrough, probably the oldest church in the county, is now all that remains after much medieval re-modelling and extensive Victorian 'restoration'. At Laughton en le Morthen the Saxon fabric in the form of a north doorway in 'Rotherham Red' sandstone is the most obvious sign of a pre-Conquest church (Figure 9.2 (a)). At Burghwallis the thickness of the walls, and the use of herring-bone stonework (see Chapter 8) and 'side alternate' quoins all point to a pre-Norman building; the tower is probably Norman. Finally, St Andrew's Church at Bolton on Dearne has a Saxon nave identified by the massive long and short angle quoins, so typical of Anglo-Saxon church building.

Among the churches in the county with Norman fabric (*c.* 1050-1190), the most attractive are Austerfield (with a carved dragon in the tympanum of the Norman south doorway); Campsall (impressive Norman tower); Hooton Pagnell (lower stage of tower, nave, south doorway); Adwick upon Dearne (rare Norman bellcote); Thorpe Salvin (ornately carved Norman font); Maltby (tower only); and Fishlake (mostly late medieval, but with a wonderfully decorated Norman doorway (Figure 9.2 (b)).

The most impressive medieval churches in South Yorkshire were those built in the Perpendicular style between 1350 and 1530. This style is characterised by its straight mullioned windows, its fan-shaped vaulting, its spaciousness and airiness, its battlements and pinnacles and its magnificent towers and spires. The best are at Bradfield, Darton, Ecclesfield, Royston and, most impressive of all, Tickhill and Rotherham (Figure 9.2 (c) and (d)).

MONASTERIES AND THEIR ESTATES

Monastic ownership of the land in medieval South Yorkshire was considerable. There was a Cistercian monastery at Roche and nunnery at Hampole, a Clunaic (later Benedictine) monastery at Monk Bretton, a Premonstratensian abbey at Beauchief and a small Benedictine priory at Ecclesfield. Nothing remains of the Hampole nunnery but remains of the other four institutions are still important features of the landscape. At Beauchief, which was founded about 1176, only the tower of the abbey church is visible together with outlines of its precincts which included woods and fishponds. At Ecclesfield a substantial part of the small priory, (originally a dependent cell of the abbey of St Wandrille in Normandy) most obviously the chapel with its undercroft, are incorporated into a private house which was sympathetically restored in 1889. At Monk Bretton, founded about 1154, the ruins are fairly complete and show clearly the monastic layout. Most notable are the gatehouse, the prior's lodging (which was converted into a house for one of the Earl of Shrewsbury's sons after the dissolution of the monasteries), a well preserved administrative building, and the massive drain from the kitchen and latrine block.

The ruins of Roche Abbey (Figure 9.3) provide the best overall picture of the setting and organisation of a monastic community. The abbey was founded in 1147 on a site given by two patrons, Richard de Busli who owned that part of the site north of Maltby Beck and Richard Fitzturgis who owned the land to the south of the beck. The site is a typical Cistercian site, tucked away in a secluded spot with a good water supply.

The name, which is Norman-French, refers to one of the rocky outcrops of Magnesian Limestone which flank the valley. The twelfth century Cistercian monks made astute use of the site. The abbey was located within a 12.5 hectare precinct bounded by a wall about 3m in height and the main complex of buildings was approached through an outer gatehouse and an inner gatehouse (of which the lower storey survives). The abbey church was sited on the north side of the valley where it enjoyed a southerly aspect. Between the church and the far side of Maltby Beck lay the chapter house, cloister and the refectories and dormitories of the monks and lay brothers (who did much of the physical labour in and around the abbey and on distant granges until about 1300), with a shared kitchen between them. The main latrine block lay athwart the beck at the eastern edge of the complex where sewage and waste would be carried away from the site. The abbot's lodging and the infirmaries for monks and lay brothers were across the beck. Beyond the abbot's lodging a tributary stream was dammed to create a fishpond.

The influence of monastic establishments was felt far beyond their precincts. They were showered with gifts of land by landowners who wanted to pave their way into heaven and until the mid-fourteenth century the monasteries directly farmed their lands and engaged in industrial enterprises through their lay brothers. After that date they rented their lands to tenants. Their outlying farms and other industrial enterprises (which could range from stone quarrying and ironstone mining and iron making, to corn milling, leather tanning, salt panning and fishing) were called granges. Beauchief Abbey had a grange at Strawberry Lee at Totley, Ecclesfield Priory had three farms within Ecclesfield parish including Woolley Grange (the present Concord Park), and Monk Bretton Priory had four granges in South Yorkshire. Roche Abbey, the richest of the South Yorkshire monasteries, had no fewer than eleven granges in South Yorkshire, three in Derbyshire (including sheep farms at One Ash and Calling Low in the White Peak), two in Lincolnshire, one in Nottinghamshire and one on the Yorkshire-Lancashire border at Rochdale.

Monastic establishments outside South Yorkshire were also major landowners and entrepreneurs in South Yorkshire. For example, Rufford Abbey in Nottinghamshire acquired the manor of Rotherham, Worksop Priory owned land at Branton and Thorpe Salvin, Bolton Abbey had lands at Wentworth, and Nostell Priory were landowners at Great Houghton, Swinton, and Thurnscoe. There were monastic granges devoted to farming belonging to monasteries from outside South Yorkshire at Bessacarr (Kirkstall Abbey), at Braithwell (Lewes

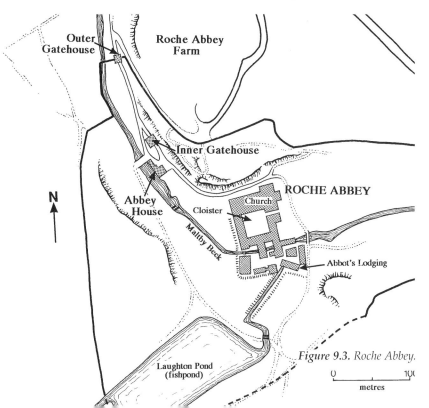

Figure 9.3. Roche Abbey.

Priory), Barnburgh (Nostell Priory), and Rossington (St Mary's Abbey, York) . In addition, some time in the twelfth century, Rievaulx Abbey obtained the rights to the ironstone and woods for making charcoal (the fuel for smelting) in the manor of Stainborough and, more famously, in 1161 Kirkstead Abbey in Lincolnshire was granted rights and land in Kimberworth and Ecclesfield by Richard de Busli and Richard de Lovetot respectively, to mine ironstone and to set up iron furnaces and forges. A late medieval building, called the Monks' Smithy Houses in the nineteenth century and renamed Kirkstead Abbey Grange in 1900, survives on what was the edge of Thorpe Common next to an ancient trans-Pennine route from Rotherham. The building contains much re-used material, probably from the original grange buildings (see Chapter 8, Figure 8.7).

POST-MEDIEVAL CHURCH AND CHAPEL BUILDING

After the Reformation, little building of Church of England churches took place until the nineteenth century. St Paul's in Sheffield, built in 1720, was an outstanding example of a Georgian church but was demolished before the Second World War. Two chapels, built by the local lord of the manor are worthy of note. At Great Houghton Sir Edward Rodes built his unusually rounded-battlemented and stepped gabled chapel in about 1650 (Figure 9.4 (a)). Ten miles to the west at Midhopestones in the Pennines on the northern edge of the extensive Ecclesfield parish Godfrey Bosville rebuilt the medieval chapel of ease (St James') in 1705. This is a tiny building constructed in local gritstone with a stone slate roof. It still contains the original pews and has a west gallery (Figure 9.4 (b)).

Nineteenth century population growth and urban and industrial expansion heralded the beginning of a long period of new church building by the established church to satisfy the demand in the rapidly expanding residential suburbs, industrial districts and in the many mining villages. Such South Yorkshire landmarks as St Mary's, Sheffield (1826-30), one of five churches built in the 1820s in Sheffield under the Million Act to aid the building of churches in rapidly growing areas, (Figure 9.4 (c)); St George's, Doncaster (1854-58, to replace the medieval church destroyed by fire in 1853, Figure 9.4 (d)); St James', Doncaster (1858, by shareholders of the great Northern Railway); Holy Trinity, Wentworth (1875-77, by Earl Fitzwilliam); and St John's, Ranmoor, Sheffield (1877-88 and described by Sir Nicholas Pevsner as 'opulent'), all belong to this period. The nineteenth and early twentieth centuries also saw the building of a number of Roman Catholic churches of which the most notable is St Marie's in Sheffield (1846-50), now the Roman Catholic cathedral for the Hallamshire diocese.

The century also saw the break-up of the old parish system in the urban and industrial areas. The parish of Sheffield, for example, was sub-divided into more than twenty ecclesiastical districts and the enormous Ecclesfield parish from which Bradfield had already been separated was further reduced in size by the creation of separate ecclesiastical districts at Chapeltown, Grenoside, High Green, Oughtibridge, Wadsley and Wincobank. There was also much re-building and restoration of existing medieval churches.

Nonconformist chapels of the second half of the eighteenth and nineteenth centuries abound in South Yorkshire, and vary from primitive cottage-like constructions to large buildings for which the word chapel seems inappropriate. Of the grander buildings, Underbank Unitarian Chapel at Stannington deserves special attention. It was built in 1742-43 in local stone with a stone-slated roof. On the main front are two tall arched windows originally ranged on either side of the pulpit. The minister's house sits close by the chapel. Both lie within a

Figure 9.4. *Examples of post-medieval church building: (a) Great Houghton Chapel (1650). (b) St James' Chapel, Midhopestones (1705). (c) St Mary's, Sheffield (1826-30). (d) St George's, Doncaster (1854-58).* The Author

graveyard planted with mature trees. Still in the Sheffield area, two other nonconformist chapels are worthy of particular note: the Upper Chapel, at the top of Norfolk Street, is notable for being the first brick building in Sheffield (1715, but refaced in stone and given its porticoed entrance in 1848); and Carver Street Methodist Church (1804) capable of holding a congregation of 1,100 and recently converted into an Australian theme pub! Many of the smaller nonconformist chapels have also become redundant through population decline and amalgamation, and where they have not been demolished, they have been converted to a multitude of other uses including industrial premises, antique centres, private residences and even theatres. Some are now used by other faiths.

VICARAGES AND SCHOOLS

Like chapels, large rectories, vicarages and nonconformist manses, built or re-built for large families and retinues of servants, lying cheek by jowl with an ancient church or large chapel, are an endangered species (Figure 9.5). Most of those surviving from before the First World War are Victorian but a minority are much earlier, the oldest being at Campsall occupying what was originally a medieval manor house. Unable to be properly maintained or adequately heated, many have been sold, and others have been demolished.

The rectory at Tankersley, lying within a medieval moat, is now a private residence and the attractive Georgian vicarage at Norton in Sheffield is up for sale. 'The Brontes of South Yorkshire', the Gattys of Ecclesfield, have suffered badly compared with their counterparts at Howarth: Ecclesfield vicarage, the home of Dr Alfred Gatty, his wife Margaret and daughter Juliana Ewing, both celebrated children's authors, has long been demolished.

Church schools are a neglected aspect of the religious

Figure 9.5. (Top) *Vicarage and All Saints' Church at Darton.*
Figure 9.6. (Bottom) *Lound National School.* Chapeltown and High Green Archive

contribution to local communities. The early ones were the result of endowments from generous benefactors. The earliest of these in South Yorkshire, built in the early seventeenth century, is at Laughton en le Morthen, across the road from the church. It is two storeys high, built of local limestone with mullioned windows. More likely to be standing and probably forming the core of bigger establishments are the schools built in the nineteenth century under the auspices of either the nonconformist British and Foreign Schools Society (founded in 1808) or the National Society for the Education of the Poor in the Principles of the Established Church (founded in 1811). By 1851 the latter society controlled over 17,000 'National Schools' throughout the country. An attractive example of a National School is Lound School at Chapeltown, Sheffield, built in 1844, and recently converted into offices (Figure 9.6).

What to read about churches in the landscape

BOTTOMLEY, F (1993) *Yorkshire Churches*, Alan Sutton.

FERGUSSON, Peter (1990), *Roche Abbey, South Yorkshire*, English Heritage.

GLISTER, R (1999) 'The Doncaster Plant churches: St James' and St Jude's in B. Elliott (Ed) *Aspects of Doncaster 2*, Wharncliffe Publishing, pp. 84-88.

HEY, D. (1979) *The Making of South Yorkshire*, chapters 5, 14, 15 and 26, Moorland Publishing.

HEY, D (1982) *Buildings of Britain 1550-1750: Yorkshire*, Moorland Publishing.

HOLLAND, D (1999) 'Jigsaws of building history: three parish churches in the Lower Don valley' in B. Elliott (Ed) *Aspects of Doncaster 2*, Wharncliffe Publishing, pp. 89-105.

PEVSNER, SIR N. (1959) *The Buildings of England, Yorkshire: The West Riding*, Pelican Books.

RYDER, P. (1982) *Saxon Churches in South Yorkshire*, South Yorkshire County Council,

WINCHESTER, A. (1990) *Discovering Parish Boundaries*, Shire Publications Ltd.

Places to visit

Medieval parish churches: Every church with medieval fabric is worth a visit. Some churches are open to the public and others can be viewed by appointment. Requests should be made to the incumbent whose telephone number is usually displayed outside the church. Failing that, Crockford's clerical directory should be consulted.

My personal top twenty are Arksey, Austerfield, Bolton upon Dearne, Bradfield, Burghwallis, Campsall, Conisbrough, Darton, Ecclesfield, Finningley, Fishlake, Hatfield, Hooton Pagnell, Laughton en le Morthen, Norton (Sheffield), Rotherham, Sprotbrough, Thorne, Tickhill, Wentworth (old church).

Among later churches and chapels, St James' Midhopestones, Underbank Chapel, Stannington, Upper Chapel, Sheffield, St Marie's RC Cathedral, Sheffield, and St George's, Doncaster are all worth a visit.

Monastic buildings: Ecclesfield Priory can be seen from Ecclesfield churchyard and the tower at Beauchief Abbey from the lane beside it. Both Monk Bretton Priory (no charge) and Roche Abbey (entrance charge) are in the guardianship of English Heritage.

PARKS AND GARDENS

PARKS ARE AS OLD as civilisation itself. They originated in ancient Assyria, Persia, India, Egypt, Greece and Rome. More than 3,000 years ago the king of Assyria boasted of parks planted with exotic trees, stocked with oxen, stags and elephants, embellished with fish ponds and beautified with complex water systems and with temples and shrines on artificially created small hills.

MEDIEVAL DEER PARKS

There were certainly parks in Anglo-Saxon England, but it was a tradition that flourished widely only after the Norman Conquest. In the Domesday Survey in 1086, twenty years after the Conquest, thirty-five deer parks were recorded; estimates of the number of parks by the year 1300 vary - one authority suggests 1,900, another puts the figure at over 3,000.

Medieval deer parks were symbols of status and wealth. They were created by kings, by the nobility and by bishops, and they were also to be found attached to monasteries, nunneries and colleges. As all deer belonged to the Crown, from the beginning of the thirteenth century it was necessary to obtain a licence from the king to create a park. A grant of *free warren* was given which gave a landowner a general right to hunt on his demesne (the land on his estate not in the hands of tenants), and this general permission was often converted into the creation of a specially enclosed area: the deer park. The medieval deer parks attached to the castles at Conisbrough and Sheffield pre-dated the issuing of royal licences and so must have been of twelfth century or even earlier - possibly Saxon - origin. There were at least 70 medieval grants of free warren in South Yorkshire and there are records of 26 deer parks. Nationally, the great age of the medieval deer park was

the century and a half between 1200 and 1350, a period of growing population and agricultural prosperity. Landowners had surplus wealth and there were still sufficient areas of waste on which to create parks. In South Yorkshire the bulk of grants of free warren and creation of parks was in the period from 1250 to 1325 when 44 out of the 70 known medieval grants were made. Significantly, no grants were made for 30 years following the Black Death (1349), but there were then 21 grants between 1379 and 1400. The latest known medieval grant of free warren/free park was in 1491-92 when Brian Sandford was granted permission to create a park at Thorpe Salvin. This grant is also notable for the fact that it was accompanied by a gift of twelve does from the king's park at Conisbrough 'towards the storing of his parc at Thorp'. Post-medieval grants of free warren were less common. In South Yorkshire such a grant was made to the 2nd Viscount Castleton in 1637 by King Charles I which led to the creation of Sandbeck Park.

Most of the grants of free warren and for emparking were to lay lords such as the locally important Fitzwilliams, Bosvilles, Chaworths and de Vavasors and also to the heads of the great Norman dynasties whose ancestors had accompanied the Conqueror to England in 1066: the de Warennes of Conisbrough Castle who had parks at Conisbrough and Hatfield, the de Furnivals of Sheffield Castle who had parks at Sheffield and Whiston and the de Buslis of Tickhill Castle who had a park at Tinsley.

Religious houses were also granted free warren and permission to create parks. Like lay owners they employed officials (bailiffs, grangers, parkers, foresters) to manage their demesnes. Some abbots and priors hunted in their parks - one of the practices indicating a pre-occupation with non-religious matters of which they were accused by Henry VIII. A contemporary record states that Richard de Wombwell, prior of Nostell Priory from 1372-85, was fond of hunting. Significantly, the priory was granted free warren in its lands at Great Houghton, Swinton and Thurnscoe during his term of office. There is still a wood called Little Park in Great Houghton. Besides Nostell Priory, other religious houses outside South Yorkshire - Rufford Abbey and Worksop Priory in Nottinghamshire and Bolton Abbey in Craven - also held rights of free warren in South Yorkshire. The local religious communities at Monk Bretton Priory, Roche Abbey and the nunnery at Hampole also had rights of free warren on their South Yorkshire properties. One of the properties of Bolton Abbey on which they had a grant of free warren was at Wentworth Woodhouse and was the antecedent of the later Wentworth Park. The prior of Worksop Priory created a park at Ryknieldthorpe (Thorpe Salvin) wood and Monk Bretton Priory created a park on its property at Rainborough in Brampton and the 18 hectare wood there is still called Rainborough Park.

The creation of a park - called emparkment - involved enclosing an area of land with a fence to keep the deer and other game in, and predators (wolves) and poachers out. The fence was called the park pale and consisted of either cleft oak stakes, often set on a bank, or a stone wall. Tankersley Park, one of the longest surviving local medieval parks, was completely surrounded by a stone wall. Park pales contained deer leaps, devices which allowed wild deer to enter the park but prevented the park herd from escaping. As parks could vary in size from under 50 hectares to a thousand or more (at its greatest extent Sheffield Park covered more than 1,000 hectares and was nearly thirteen kilometres in circumference) fencing was a major initial and recurring expense. Because of

this, the most economical shape for a deer park was a circle or a rectangle with rounded corners. Figure 10.1 shows the outlines of the medieval parks at Aston, Sheffield and Tankersley.

Deer parks were not primarily created for hunting for pleasure, although hunting did take place there. The first known documentary reference to Tankersley Park after its creation was in a law suit of 1527 when the owner, Henry Savile, was recorded as having been 'hunting at dere wythe hounds in hys parke of Tankersley'. Besides their status symbol role, their main function was to provide for their owners a reliable source of food for the table, and supplies of wood and timber: they were, therefore, an integral part of the local farming economy.

The deer in most parks were fallow deer, which are not

Figure 10.1. Boundaries of the medieval deer parks at Aston, Sheffield and Tankersley showing their rounded outlines.

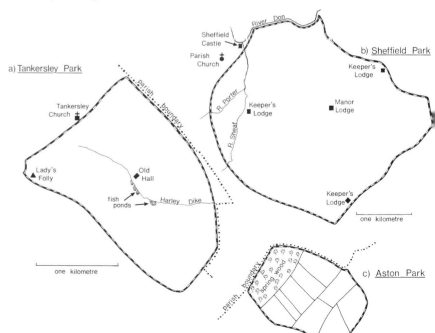

native to Britain but were probably introduced by the Normans. Fallow deer are much easier to contain within a park than the native red deer and roe deer. Locally both fallow and red deer were kept in parks. In John Harrison's survey of the Manor of Sheffield in 1637, the park there was said to be 'not meanly furnished with fallow Deare, the number of them at present is one Thousand'. Nearly a century later when Daniel Defoe rode through Tankersley Park he commented that he had seen '...the largest red deer that, I believe, are in this part of Europe: One of the hinds, I think, was larger than my horse...'. There was still a herd of more than 50 red deer at Tankersley in the 1850s when they were relocated at Wentworth due to the reduction in the size of the park because of ironstone mining. Besides deer, wild swine, hares, rabbits (also introduced by the Normans and kept in burrows in artificially made mounds) and game birds were kept in medieval parks). Herds of cattle and flocks of sheep were also kept. Another important feature of medieval deer parks were fish ponds to provide an alternative to meat in Lent and on fast days.

Although there are records of parks without trees, deer parks usually consisted of woodland and areas largely cleared of trees. The park livestock could graze in the open areas and find cover in the wooded areas. The cleared areas were called *launds* or *plains* and consisted of grassland or heath with scattered trees. Most of the trees in the launds would have been pollards, i.e., trees cut at least two metres from the ground leaving a massive lower trunk called a bolling above which a continuous crop of new growth sprouted out of reach of the grazing deer, sheep and cattle. John Evelyn in his book *Sylva*, first published in the second half of the seventeenth century, recorded some massive pollards in the deer park at Sheffield. For example he recorded one oak tree in the park whose trunk was 13 feet (4 metres) in diameter and another 10

yards (over 9 metres) in circumference. In the launds regeneration of trees was restricted because of continuous grazing and new trees were only able to grow in the protection of thickets of hawthorn and holly. Some of these unpollarded trees might reach a great age and size and were much sought after for major building projects.

Evelyn recorded a large oak tree felled in Sheffield Park that was so big when it was lying on its side that two men on opposite sides on horseback could not see each other's hats! Even more impressive was his report that in an open area within the park called Conduit Plaine there was another oak tree whose boughs were so far spreading that he estimated (giving all his calculations) that 251 horses could stand in its shade.

The woods within medieval deer parks were managed in different ways. Some were holted. A holt consisted of single stemmed trees grown for timber, rather like a modern plantation. Most woods, however, were managed as coppices, in South Yorkshire usually as coppices with standards. Deer

Figure 10.2. *Typical features of a medieval deer park.*

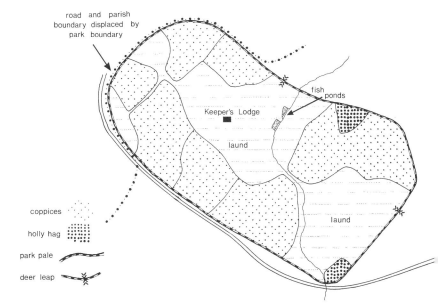

parks also contained *holly hags*, compartments composed mainly of holly that was cut for winter feed for the deer. Coppice woods within parks would have been surrounded by banks surmounted by hedges or by stone walls to protect them, during the early years of growth after the last felling, from grazing deer and rabbits and any other herbivores kept within the park. Once well grown the livestock would be allowed into the woods.

To summarise, most medieval deer parks comprised of a series of compartments: periodically or permanently fenced holts, coppices and holly hags, together with permanently

Figure 10.3. Tankersley Park c. 1730, viewed from the east. The road in the foreground is the modern A6135. Features include its boundary stone wall, Elizabethan hall, fishponds, and walled paddocks. The wood on the extreme right-hand (northern) boundary was a holly hag, and still survives as Bull Wood which is full of holly. The alignment of Tankersley parish church just outside the park boundary has been changed from east-west to north-south by the artist.

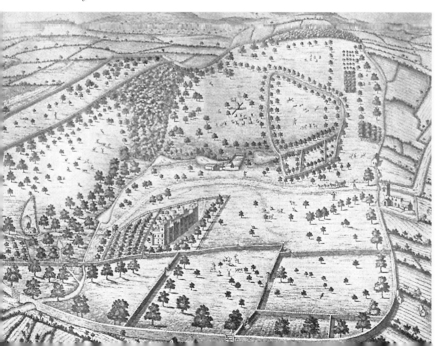

open launds or plains which might be treeless glades or dotted with thickets and pollards and other ancient trees. Man-made pillow mounds containing rabbit warrens would have almost certainly occupied part of one of the launds. There would also usually have been fishponds. Figure 10.2 shows these characteristic features in simplified form. And finally, occupying the centre of the park or elsewhere commanding wide views, would have been a parker's lodge. Large parks might have had several. Sheffield Park had three keepers' lodges as shown in Figure 10.1. Figure 10.3 shows Tankersley Park in the second decade of the eighteenth century when it still had all the characteristics of a medieval deer park.

THE DECLINE OF THE MEDIEVAL PARK AND THE RISE OF THE LANDSCAPED PARK

Between the late fifteenth and eighteenth centuries many surviving medieval parks either changed their function and hence their appearance, or ceased to be parks at all. John Speed's map of the West Riding of Yorkshire published in 1610 shows only nine surviving deer parks in South Yorkshire at Wortley, Tankersley, Brierley, Sheffield, Kimberworth, Thrybergh, Conisbrough, Treeton and Aston. Of these only Tankersley Park has survived to the present day in any recognisable form (its boundary can be walked and the fishponds still survive). Where a landlord was absent (his main country seat may have been in another county) or where his hall lay some distance from his medieval park, there was an increased possibility that the park might disappear altogether, the process being called disparkment. Well wooded parks often simply became large coppice woods, as locally was the case at Hesley Park, Cowley Park and Tinsley Park. By the time of John Harrison's survey of the manor of Sheffield in 1637, Hesley Park and Cowley Park, between Thorpe Hesley and Chapeltown, which together constituted one of the medieval parks of the de Mountenay family of Cowley, were coppice woods of 163 and 135 acres respectively, although they still contained red deer. Tinsley Park was another medieval deer park that had lost its former function by the mid-seventeenth century. In 1657 it was let by its then owner, the 2nd Earl of Strafford of Wentworth Woodhouse, to Lyonel Copley, the ironmaster, for felling for charcoal making. It then covered over 400 acres and comprised ten coppice woods and three holts. Other parks simply reverted to farmland. The medieval park at Aston had become part of Old Park Farm by 1775 and had been largely divided up into small enclosures. Even though Sheffield Park still contained 1,000 fallow deer in 1637, 971 of its 2,462 acres had been let to tenants. In the case of Kimberworth Park the first steps leading to the park's eventual total disparkment had taken place by 1649 when a farm of

about 140 acres was carved out of it. By 1671 the whole of the park had been leased, the farm as in 1649, and the rest, amounting to over 600 acres, to a local ironmaster whose main interest was in the ironstone and coal that could be mined and the coppice woods that could be felled and made into charcoal. By 1732 the whole of the former park had been divided into farms (Figure 10.4).

While hundreds of medieval parks were disappearing, many others took on a new lease of life and new parks were created because the concept of the park was changing. Its primary function changed from being a game preserve and source of wood and timber to being the adornment to a country house (Figure 10.5). New residences were built within the boundaries of existing parks which were often extended and completely new landscaped parks were created. The concept of the park as an aesthetic extension of the country seat and garden began in the Tudor period and has gone through many fashions in the last 500 years. Some of the greatest changes and new creations occurred in the eighteenth

Figure 10.4. *The former Kimberworth Deer Park, 1732. By that date the park had been completely disparked and converted into a series of farms.*

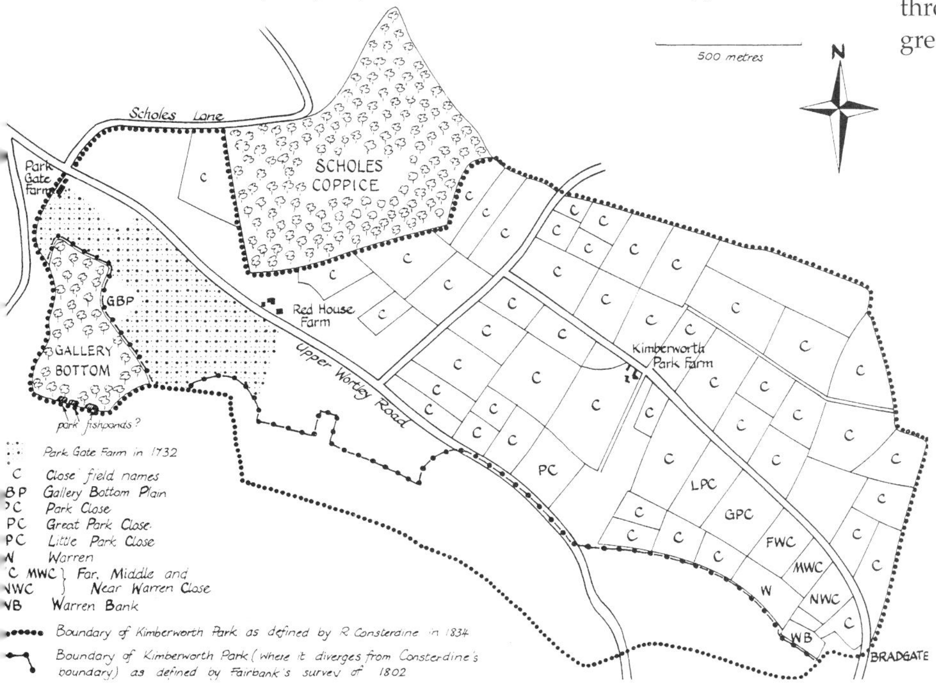

Figure 10.5. *The park at Wentworth Woodhouse with the mansion in the background as portrayed in an early nineteenth century engraving.*

century under the influence of landscape designers such as John Vanbrugh, Charles Bridgeman, William Kent, Lancelot 'Capability' Brown, Humphrey Repton and Richard Woods. The demesnes at Wentworth Woodhouse (Figure 10.5) and Sandbeck Park were remodelled in this period. Other parks in South Yorkshire laid out around country houses in the eighteenth and nineteenth centuries include those at Cannon Hall, Brodsworth, Cusworth and The Oaks at Norton (then part of Derbyshire).

On a more intimate level, gardens were created both for pleasure and to provide fruit and vegetables for the big house, and the ones at Wentworth Woodhouse, Wentworth Castle, Cannon Hall, Brodsworth and Whinfell (Sheffield) are open to the public. Wentworth Woodhouse still has its 'hot walls' (now part of the garden centre), a sunken Japanese garden created in the eighteenth and early nineteenth centuries, and a grotto

Figure 10.6. The framework of a magnificent rock garden recently revealed at Brodsworth Hall. The Author

containing a bear pit. The garden at Wentworth Castle is a magnificent woodland garden containing national collections of rhododendrons and magnolias and notable collections of azaleas and Himalayan poppies. Each woodland compartment is linked to the next by woodland walks or wide sweeps of lawn with nearly 30 romantic follies. The main attraction at Cannon Hall is the kitchen garden whose walls are filled with espalier trained pear trees, some said to be nearly 200 years old. One of the greenhouses in the kitchen garden contains the Cannon Hall muscat vine, about 150 years old.

Another part of the Cannon Hall gardens contains a lily pool framed by romantically decaying and ivy-covered gothic masonry and window tracery. The Victorian gardens at Brodsworth are still undergoing restoration following the opening of the house to the public in 1995. One of Brodsworth's glories is a magnificent rockery garden (Figure 10.6) which has been revealed from beneath a jungle of weeds. It is currently being re-planted. Whinfell Quarry Gardens, next to Whirlow Brook Park in south-western Sheffield, were once the gardens of a house called Whinfell built for the industrialist Samuel Doncaster in 1900. The house was destroyed by fire in 1971 but the gardens survive. They contain specimen trees such as weeping beech, western hemlock, cedar and Japanese maples, and many other shrubs and alpines, including giant gunneras (Chilean rhubarb).

MUNICIPAL PARKS

The parks described so far were private and predominantly rural. At the beginning of the nineteenth century only London had large urban parks - the royal parks - Hyde Park, Green Park, St James' Park, Kensington Gardens and Regent's Park - and these were gradually opened to the public through entrance fees. Selective opening hours were used to restrict entry on occasions.

All the urban parks in South Yorkshire are the legacy of the Victorian park movement. The need for managed green spaces in Britain for the general public was gradually identified in the first three decades of the nineteenth century as the country rapidly urbanised and urban centres multiplied in number and spread outwards, consuming large areas of formerly rural land and leaving the urban populations - there was no public transport system to speak of - increasingly distant from country lanes and footpaths and un-industrialised riversides.

The rate of population growth and urbanisation in Victorian Britain was extremely high. In 1801 the population of England and Wales was 9.2 million. One hundred years later it was 32 million - a growth rate over the century of nearly 350 per cent. Not only did the population grow rapidly, it was increasingly concentrated in urban areas. In 1801 only 19 per cent of the population lived in places with a population of over 20,000; by 1851, 54 per cent of the population was classified as urban, and by 1911 the figure was 80 per cent.

It must also be remembered that the urban populations - especially in the rapidly growing ports and industrial towns and cities - were overwhelmingly youthful and birth rates were high. There was no compulsory education until 1870 and adults and children alike among the working classes worked long hours in mines and factories. After work they returned to densely packed housing areas where infectious diseases spread rapidly.

It was to these populations and these types of area that the early park promoters turned their attention. They stressed the physical and social benefits of parks. Their motives, however, were not wholly selfless. It was argued that areas where the working classes could take supervised exercise in their 'spare' time (preferably in family groups) in a parkland atmosphere would lead to a healthy workforce, promote stable families and dampen down unrest and militancy at work.

Figure 10.7. Locke Park, Barnsley, opened in 1862, through donations of land and money by the widow of Joseph Locke, the railway engineer. The map shows the layout of the park and the photograph shows the observation tower erected in 1877. Photograph courtesy of Chris Sharpe,'Old Barnsley'

Official recognition of the need for parks dates from 1833 when the Select Committee on Public Walks presented its report to Parliament. The report established that needs were greatest in Birmingham, Leeds, Liverpool and Manchester. London, of course, had its royal parks, although provision in the East End of London was poor. The report did not distinguish between public open space and semi-public open space (eg., botanical gardens where only subscribers could visit at any time, and the general public was only allowed in on certain occasions) so the situation was even worse than they had painted.

In the decade following publication of the Select Committee report several new parks were created. Preston has the distinction of being the first industrial town to create a municipal park - Moor Park created by the enclosure of a common in 1833. In 1841 the Duke of Norfolk donated land for Norfolk Park in Sheffield - but this was for use of the land only and the City Council did not acquire the site itself until 1909. Another early park in Sheffield is the Botanical Gardens, opened in 1836 and laid out in the Gardenesque style by

Robert Marnock with small scale garden landscapes connected by curvilinear paths and expanses of grass with specimen trees in imitation of a landscaped park. An important feature of the newly opened garden was its magnificent conservatories with a frontage of 100 yards (92 metres). Admission was originally restricted to shareholders and subscribers except four gala days when the general public was admitted.

It is often easy to identify a Victorian park simply from its name - look for a royal connection: Victoria Park, Queen's Park, Albert Park, Prince's Park - or the name of a local benefactor - the Duke of Norfolk and Mark Firth in Sheffield and the Locke family in Barnsley (Figure 10.7).

It was not until the Towns Improvement Clauses Act of 1847 that local authorities could buy or rent land specifically for recreation without a local act of Parliament and they were still not allowed to maintain through the rates land they had been given for park development. The passing of the 10 Hour Act (length of the working day) and the Saturday Half Holiday Movement provided a further stimulus to the municipal park movement and this was reinforced by the 1859 Recreation Grounds Act, which encouraged the donation of money and land for park development, and the 1860 Public Improvements Act which gave local authorities the power to acquire and manage parks out of the rates. These Acts inspired a further flurry of donations and park creations in the 1860s and 1870s. Locke Park in Barnsley (Figure 10.7) and Firth Park and Weston Park in Sheffield date from this period. After 1875 and the passing of the Public Health Act, which allowed local authorities to raise government loans to develop parks, there was a further rapid increase in the number of urban parks, including Boston Park, Rotherham (1876), Clifton Park, Rotherham (1891), and Victoria Park, Rawmarsh (1901).

Figure 10.8. Boston Park, Rotherham, opened in 1876. Part of the park was once a quarry, the face of which skirts the main footpath. This part of the park also contains the old doorway of the College of Jesus, a house for chantry priests which stood near the parish church and which was dissolved by Henry VIII in 1547.

The newest municipal parks are called country parks. When they were 'invented' in the 1960s they were designed to introduce people to the countryside in a managed recreational environment, and to act as 'interceptors' between townspeople and areas of outstanding beauty such as the Peak District which were thought to be in danger of being over-run by the increasingly affluent, car-owning population. Like the Victorian parks before them, large new parks are distributed in the urban fringe wherever land has become available whether in the form of a redundant reservoir and its surrounding land as at Thrybergh (Figure 10.10) and Ulley country parks in Rotherham and Worsbrough Country Park in Barnsley, a land reclamation site as at Rother Valley, a large wood as at Howell Country Park at Clayton (Doncaster) or the landscaped grounds of a big house as at Cannon Hall in Barnsley and Cusworth and Highfields (Adwick le Street) in Doncaster.

Figure 10.9. The opening of Firth Park in 1875 by the Prince of Wales.

When the parks were opened - often by royalty - crowds were immense (Figure 10.9). And after they were opened they were very heavily used. By the last decade of the nineteenth century the Victorian parks movement had changed the face of Britain's towns and cities. But the amount, pattern and type of park provision varied from one urban area to another. It would take the introduction of planning legislation, the injection of new ideas on physical planning and the consideration in more detail of specific needs before provision was rationalised.

Figure 10.10. Thrybergh Country Park developed on and around an old reservoir.

What to read about parks and gardens

BEASTALL, T. W. (1995) 'Sandbeck Hall and Park', pp. 89-98 in M. Jones (Ed) *Aspects of Rotherham 1*, Wharncliffe Publishing.

CARDER, J. (1986) *The Sheffield Botanical Gardens, a short history*, Sheffield City Council.

CONWAY, H. (1991) *People's Parks*, Cambridge University Press.

HEY, D. (1975) ' The Parks at Tankersley and Wortley', *Yorkshire Archaeological Journal*, Volume 47, pp. 109-119.

JONES, M. (1996) ' The medieval deer park at Kimberworth', pp. 115-135 in M. Jones (Ed) *Aspects of Rotherham 2*, Wharncliffe Publishing.

JONES, M. (1996) Deer in South Yorkshire: an Historical Perspective, *Journal of Practical Ecology and Conservation*, Special Publication No 1, pp. 11-26.

LASDUN, S. (1992) *The English Park: Royal, Private & Public*, The Vendome Press.

LEMMON, K. (1978) *The Gardens of Britain, 5: Yorkshire and Humberside*, Batsford (in association with the Royal Horticultural Society).

SEWELL, J. (1997) 'Paradise lost? Sheffield's Historic Parks and Gardens', pp. 203-225 in M. Jones (Ed) *Aspects of Sheffield 1*, Wharncliffe Publishing.

RACKHAM, O. (1986) *The History of the Countryside*, Chapter 6, Dent.

ROGERS, A. (1998) 'Deer parks in the Maltby Area', pp. 8-30 in M. Jones (Ed) *Aspects of Rotherham 3*, Wharncliffe Publishing.

Places to visit

It is still possible to walk most of the medieval boundary of **Tankersley** deer park and view the ruined Elizabethan mansion in the park. The landscaped park at **Wentworth Woodhouse** still has a herd of red deer.   The park at **Cannon Hall,** now a country park, still has its serpentine lake, mature park trees and a ha-ha separating the park from the house and gardens.

The gardens at **Cannon Hall, Wentworth Woodhouse** and **Whinfell Quarry** are open to the public on most days of the year, and there are tours of the garden at **Wentworth Castle** in May. Parts of the gardens at **Brodsworth Hall** are still being restored; they are open to the public on those days when the house is open.

Weston Park in Sheffield, **Locke Park** in Barnsley, **Boston Park,** and **Clifton Park** in Rotherham and **Victoria Park** in Rawmarsh are all good examples of Victorian municipal parks. **The Sheffield Botanical Gardens,** which is currently the subject of a major restoration project, is an outstanding example of its type. There are leaflets available about all the country parks named in the text and there are full programmes of events throughout the year.

THE IMPACT OF INDUSTRY ON THE LANDSCAPE

THE IMPACT OF INDUSTRY on the South Yorkshire landscape has been long-term, extremely varied and complex. Sites have been successively occupied, abandoned, re-used and, particularly in the last three decades of the twentieth century, masked, altered or obliterated altogether. Nowhere is this obliteration of a long-developed industrial landscape more evident than in the Dearne valley between Hoyland and Conisbrough where large-scale re-contouring, landscaping, and the development of a new road transport network have created a largely new landscape. Yet much evidence remains across the county of its industrial past. The chapter concentrates on the impact of the exploitation of the county's rivers, woods and coal resources, and on the iron, steel and linen textile industries. More could have been written about stone quarrying, leather tanning, nail making, pottery and glass, all once important industries, but lack of space prohibits this. These omissions are redressed to some extent in the guide to further reading and the list of interesting places to visit at the end of the chapter.

FUEL AND POWER: EXPLOITATION OF WATER, WOODS AND COAL RESOURCES
Harnessing water power
Water power in South Yorkshire in the popular mind is primarily associated with Sheffield and with the cutlery industry, particularly the grinding phase (putting on a cutting edge) of that industry. But that greatly simplifies the picture. Water power was used much more widely geographically in the past and provided the power for a wide range of industries including iron forging, corn milling, scythe making, paper making, bark crushing (at a tannery), cloth fulling, lead smelting and snuff making.

Figure 11.1. A nineteenth century print of a water-powered site on one of Sheffield's rivers. The dam (reservoir) is feeding an overshot waterwheel. The rest of the scene is over-romanticised. Working conditions were most unhealthy. Grinders in particular were exposed to major health hazards. The main cause of death among grinders was 'grinders' asthma' caused by the inhalation of stone and metal dust. In the 1830s life expectancy among fork grinders, who ground 'dry', was 28-32 years.

The first water-powered mills, for grinding corn, were probably established in the early thirteenth century. Records are patchy throughout the medieval period, especially in the Sheffield area but sites were widespread by the beginning of the sixteenth century. There were about 50 water-powered industrial sites on Sheffield's rivers by 1660, the number had risen to about 90 by 1740, and this had increased to about 130 by the end of the eighteenth century, after which only a handful of new sites were created. At the height of the use of water-power on Sheffield's rivers they occurred on average four times in every mile of river. Beyond the Don and its tributaries as many as 52 water-powered sites have been identified on the River Dearne and its tributaries in South Yorkshire, and on Maltby Dike, a minor tributary of the River Ryton, itself only a tributary of the Idle, nine medieval water-powered sites have been identified.

The usual method of harnessing water power in South Yorkshire was that a weir was built to deflect water from the river into a reservoir, locally called a dam, via a channel called a head goit or leat. The dam was parallel to the river but at a higher level. Water was fed from the dam onto a vertical water wheel and then flowed away, via a tail goit, to rejoin the river downstream. Where the fall of water was over about 2.5 metres, an overshot wheel was normal, with the water hitting the wheel close to the top (Figure 11.1). Where the fall of water was lower a breast wheel would be used, with the water feeding it lower down. Very low falls of water fed undershot wheels with the stream normally flowing directly under the wheel. Many water-powered sites survive (see places to visit at the end of the chapter).

Charcoal and whitecoal

The preparation of charcoal for use as the fuel for iron smelting is the oldest recorded woodland industry in the Sheffield region. In a deed dated 1161, Richard de Busli, the lord of the manor of Kimberworth, granted the right to Kirkstead Abbey in Lincolnshire to mine, smelt and forge iron in Kimberworth. In the deed, which is in Latin, de Busli specifically gave the monks permission to collect dead wood in Kimberworth to fuel their smelting hearths - *...mortuum nemus de Kymberworth quantum sufficit illis quatuor ignibus...* (...enough dead wood from Kimberworth for all four furnaces...). The wood would not have been used in the form that it was collected but would have been converted into charcoal ('coaled') first.

Among medieval documents referring to charcoal making in South Yorkshire two are worthy of special note. In 1462 two local men, John Cotes and John Parker, were given permission to 'cole' the underwood in a number of places in the Gleadless Valley, including the present-day Rollestone Wood, where traces of charcoal making sites have survived, and in 1496 the Abbot of Beauchief Abbey gave permission to Roger Eyre to fell the coppice in Hutcliffe Wood and to convert it into charcoal for use in iron smelting at a bloom hearth, a primitive iron smelting furnace.

A list of the Earl of Shrewsbury's South Yorkshire coppice woods, written sometime between 1598-1616, explicitly states that they were woods belonging to the Earl's forges, suggesting that their most important product was charcoal. Forty-three woods are listed in the manors of Sheffield, Ecclesfield, Handsworth, Tankersley, Kimberworth, Rotherham, Whiston and Treeton and a number of them are stated to be 'coalable' or 'redie to be coled'.

Surviving records show that in the seventeenth and eighteenth centuries South Yorkshire coppice wood owners were entering into long term contracts with local ironmasters seeking supplies of charcoal. For example, in 1657 Lyonel Copley, a Rotherham ironmaster, entered into a contract with the 2nd Earl of Strafford of Wentworth Woodhouse which covered thirteen woods over a ten year period. Under the contract Copley was to cut 1,000 cords of wood (a pile of wood four feet by four feet by eight feet) each year for charcoal making. The deed deals in great detail with the cutting of the underwood and the collecting of the turves and dust for sealing the charcoal stacks.

The 1st Marquis of Rockingham (died 1750), a descendant of the the Earl of Strafford, was in the fortunate position of having both ironstone and extensive woodlands on his estate and he linked the mining of the former with the charcoaling of the latter. This policy was helped by the fact that Chapeltown furnace, which was on land leased from the Duke of Norfolk, stood just down the hill from the Marquis' Tankersley estate which contained the easily mined Tankersley ironstone. In 1745 the Marquis wrote in his rental book:

...and whereas it is the Iron Men that keep up the Price of the Wood, Especiall care must be taken that the Iron Stone be never let for a longer time than the Woods are agreed for, because as none of the Duke of Norfolk's Estate affords Iron Stone nor none other nearer than Rockley the Duke's Works at Chappel Town cannot be wrought but with the Iron Stone of Tankersley by which Advantage if care be taken thereof they must be obliged to give a good Price for the Woods for the Sake of having the said Iron Stone...

Although the market for charcoal as the fuel for iron smelting gradually disappeared during the eighteenth century with the introduction and spread of the use of coke, some markets remained and others expanded in South Yorkshire. Most importantly, charcoal was used in making blister steel in so-called cementation furnaces where successive layers of bar iron interbedded with layers of charcoal were heated up to high temperatures for up to eight days. Over 250 such furnaces with their characteristic conical chimneys were built in the Sheffield area of which only one remains in its complete state at the former Daniel Doncaster works in Hoyle Street. Another

industry based on charcoal present in the region was gunpowder manufacture which used charcoal from alder, willow and alder buckthorn trees. In the nineteenth century there were works at Worsbrough Dale and at Wharncliffe. Charcoal was also used as blacking by moulders in iron foundries and the last known charcoal burner in the Sheffield area, William Ogden of Charlton Brook near Chapeltown, who died in 1911, was employed by Newton Chambers to produce charcoal for their foundries at Thorncliffe for this purpose.

During the coaling season, which usually lasted from April to November, charcoal burners, or wood colliers as they were earlier called, lived a solitary life, often with their families about them, deep in the woodlands (Figure 11.2). Their work consisted of burning stacked lengths of coppice poles in the

Figure 11.2. Charcoal making. This would have been a familiar scene in many of South Yorkshire's woods for centuries. The wood collier's assistant is barrowing four foot lengths of wood to the charcoaling site. The wood collier is maintaining a vigil over the charcoal stack. This went on night and day for anything from seven to eleven days, hence the hut on the left. On the extreme right are sacks of charcoal waiting to be transported from the site. From a painting by John William Buxton Knight (private collection)

absence of enough air for complete combustion. The moisture was driven off during the early part of the process followed by volatile elements such as tar and creosote. The process left behind a residue of black carbon in solid form together with a little ash.

The spot where the burning took place, which was called a pitstead or hearth or platform, was about 15 feet in diameter and from it the turf was removed. Detailed research by Dr Paul Ardron has identified a substantial number of different types of site, almost all being a variation on either the 'hearth' type, in the form of a shallow bowl shape with low surrounding banks, or the 'platform' type, where a level surface is constructed on a slope by excavating the soil and throwing it forward so that the platform has a low bank at the back and a corresponding one at the front. The stack was constructed on the hearth or platform by stacking cordwood lengths (billets four feet long), on end and facing inwards, around a central triangle of wood or stake. This was continued until a stack was built up about fifteen feet in diameter and about five feet high in the shape of an inverted pudding basin. The wood was then covered by straw, grass, bracken and turves which were in their turn covered by dust and ashes. Red hot charcoal and a few dry sticks were dropped down the central flue. Once assured that the stack was alight, the wood collier sealed the flue and the fire would spread throughout the stack. It was important that the stack burned steadily and that the fire did not burn through. For this reason the charcoal burner had to be in constant attendance, protecting his charge from sudden wind changes with hurdle fencing and sacking and closing any gaps in the stack with bracken, turf and soil.

Burns lasted from two to ten days depending on size, weather conditions and the greenness of the wood. At first the stack emitted clouds of white smoke, which gradually turned to a blue haze and then died away altogether. When the burn was over, the stack was uncovered with a rake, allowed to cool and then packed in sacks or panniers.

It has already been emphasised that charcoal burners had to live more or less on top of their work and this could lead to fatal accidents. The only obvious remaining physical evidence of charcoal making in local woods is the monument to the wood collier who was burned to death in Ecclesall Woods.

Alongside charcoal making in local woods between the last quarter of the sixteenth century and the middle of the eighteenth century was another woodland industry also making a fuel for smelting ore. This time the ore was lead and the fuel was called whitecoal. A number of landowners in the south-west of the county including the Earls of Shrewsbury, the Strelleys of Beauchief and Ecclesall and the Brights of Ecclesall and Whirlow, are known to have been very active in the lead trade during that period. They obtained ore from the Derbyshire Peak District, smelted it in water-powered smelters called ore-hearths near their Coal Measure oakwoods and then transported the lead to the Humber for sale in the London market. In 1649 a lead merchant leased Ecclesall Woods in Sheffield for a 30 year period to make charcoal and whitecoal. He also rented two disused lead smelting mills next to the wood, probably on Limb Brook and the other on the Sheaf on the site of the Abbeydale Industrial Museum.

No one, as far as I know, has ever seen any whitecoal. It has not been made for over 200 years and is not likely to have survived or be recognised if it has. It was small lengths of wood, say six inches by two inches, dried in a kiln until all the moisture was driven out. William Linnard, in his book *Welsh Woods and Forests,* says that charcoal and whitecoal were mixed together in lead smelting because 'charcoal made too violent a fire, and wood alone was too gentle'. The former presence of whitecoal making in a local wood is betrayed by the presence of characteristic depressions already described in Chapter 6.

Coal mining

The first collieries were in operation in the medieval period where coal lay at a short distance below the surface in the western third of the coalfield (see cross-section on Figure 11.4). They were either bell pits, or adits or drifts (hillside tunnels) or relatively shallow shaft mines and were small and widespread. By about 180 years ago much of the easily obtained outcrop coal had been removed and as the coal seams dipped eastwards it became necessary to sink deeper shafts to reach the coal. Since that time deep shaft mines have become the usual means of obtaining coal, although during the Second World War shallow coal seams which had survived deep shaft mining have been worked by opencast methods (Figure 11.3 (A) to (C)). Figure 11.4 shows the development of the South Yorkshire coalfield at the end of the 1960s. At that time 50,000 miners were employed at more than 50 collieries producing 30 per cent of the British coal output. The first thing to note is that in 1969 there were no collieries on the Lower Coal Measures in the western part of the coalfield, where the coal had been

B.

Figure 11.3. *Differing coal mining techniques: A. Thorncliffe Drift mine which closed in 1955 after about a century of working. B. Rockingham Colliery and its coke ovens, a typical nineteenth century deep shaft colliery. C. Opencast mining at Thorncliffe in the 1980s revealing bell pit mining in the exposed coal seam.* Chapeltown and High Green Archive

A.

C.

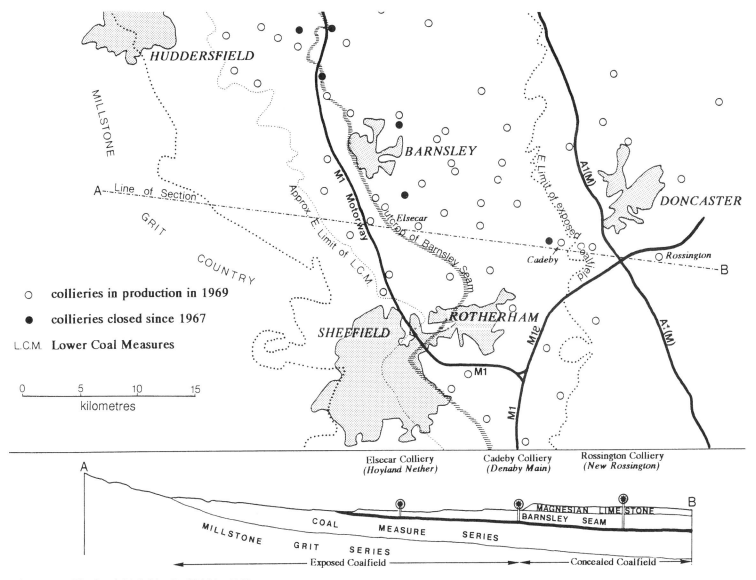

Figure 11.4. The South Yorkshire Coalfield in 1969.

removed early in the coalfield's history. Most of the collieries in 1969 lay in the Middle Coal Measures of the exposed coalfield and had mostly been sunk in the second half of the nineteenth century when the main attraction had been the nearly three metres-thick Barnsley seam, an excellent coking coal. From 1908 collieries were sunk on the concealed coalfield. Here the coal seams are far below ground and deep shafts had to be sunk. Because of the expense of sinking these collieries they were designed to work much bigger areas underground than their counterparts on the exposed coalfield, hence their smaller number and wider spacing.

Today there are only two working collieries in South Yorkshire at Maltby and Rossington and much of the evidence of past mining activity on the exposed coalfield has been swept away in an attempt to present a new image of the area to the outside world in order to attract investment and create employment. It is now necessary to travel outside South Yorkshire to Caphouse Colliery near Huddersfield to visit a mining museum and travel underground to see working conditions. Ironically it is evidence of the very earliest mining activity in the form of bell pits which has survived longest in the landscape.

IRON MANUFACTURE

Iron making is probably the oldest manufacturing industry in South Yorkshire. Evidence of ironmaking was found in an industrial annexe outside the Roman fort at Templeborough (see Figure 7.4) and as pointed earlier in this chapter the monks of Kirkstead Abbey in Lincolnshire acquired the right to mine for ironstone and to make and forge iron at Kimberworth in the second half of the twelfth century. Ironstone occurs widely on the South Yorkshire coalfield, the best known seam being the Tankersley Ironstone. The ore was mined from bell pits near the outcrop from earliest times until the second half of the

nineteenth century (Figure 11.5). Deep shaft mines were also sunk but they could not compete with more easily mined ore in places such as North Lincolnshire and ironstone mining ceased in South Yorkshire in the 1880s.

Figure 11.5. Bell pits in Tankersley Park in 1840 working the Swallow Wood Ironstone for Elsecar Ironworks. Wentworth Woodhouse Muniments in Sheffield Archives

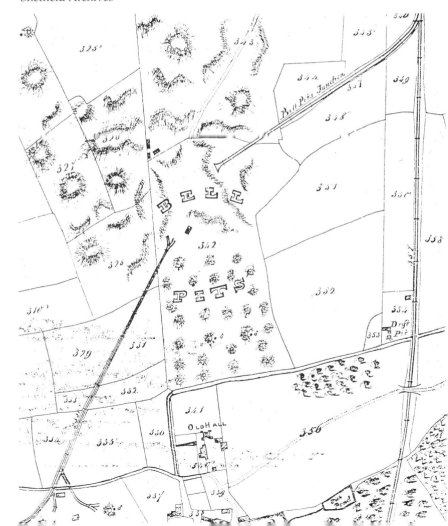

Charcoal fuelled blast furnaces were introduced into South Yorkshire in the late sixteenth century to supersede the primitive bloomeries and by the middle of the eighteenth century there were blast furnaces at Barnby, Rockley, Chapeltown and Masbrough surrounded by bell-pit ironstone workings and coppice woods which supplied charcoal for fuel. Each furnace was associated with a forge located on the bank of a river where there was a considerable volume of water:

Wortley, Wadsley, Attercliffe, Masbrough and Kilnhurst forges were on the Don and the Stainborough forge was on the Dove, a tributary of the Dearne. In the late eighteenth and early nineteenth centuries new coke fuelled blast furnaces were established at Thorncliffe, Hoyland, Elsecar and Parkgate, at what were to become large centres of production (see Figure 11.6).

The production of pig iron gave rise to a thriving wrought and cast iron industry quite distinct from the Sheffield light

Figure 11.6. *Thorncliffe Ironworks in 1876, dominated by its two blast furnaces. Note the ranges of coke ovens surrounding the works.* Chapeltown and High Green Archive

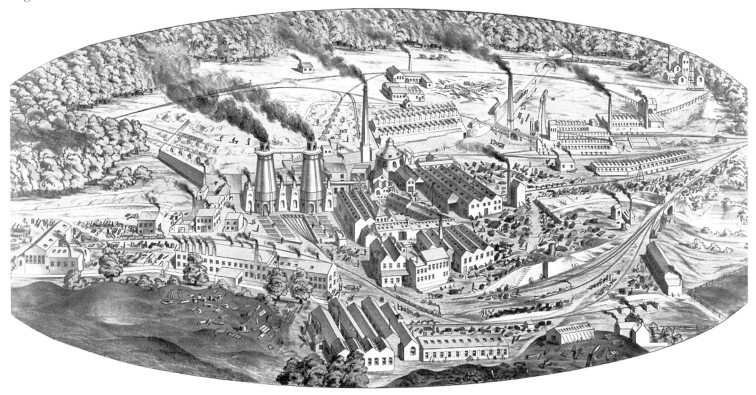

steel trades and heavy and special steels industry (Figure 11.7). The railway engineering industry, centred largely on Rotherham, replaced ordnance manufacture as the mainstay of that town's economy in the first phase of the railway age, and foundries producing machinery for the textile industry replaced wire drawing in Barnsley. At Thorncliffe, gas appliances and gas plant manufacture became important product lines in the nineteenth century, and Rotherham and Sheffield became important centres of the grate, range and decorative cast iron industry. In the second half of the nineteenth century the railway engineering industry spread to Doncaster in the shape of the locomotive and carriage repair works of the Great Northern Railway, established at Hexthorpe in 1851, which transformed Doncaster from a market town to an important industrial centre and created a completely new industrial and residential area.

Figure 11.7. Rolling wrought iron plate at John Brown's Atlas Works, Sheffield in 1861.

Little of this iron industry remains, either in production or in the form of preserved industrial sites (see list of places to visit at the end of the chapter).

STEEL MAKING IN SHEFFIELD

Although local supplies of charcoal for fuel and sandstone for grindstones were important factors in the early growth of the steel industry in Sheffield, the most powerful locational factor was water power, and until the eighteenth century this gave rise to a scattered industry along the valley of the Don and its tributaries the Loxley, Porter, Rivelin, Sheaf, and Blackburn Brook. The industry was already well established in the medieval period and, as has already been pointed out, there were about 50 water-powered sites on Sheffield's rivers by 1660 and the number had risen 90 by 1740, the majority involved in some aspect of steel making and the manufacture of steel edge tools. Many of these sites, as discussed above, still survive in some form today. After about 1750 coke instead of charcoal was used for making steel (using Huntsman's crucible process, invented in 1744) and towards the end of the century steam engines began to replace water wheels, but this was a slow process.

Nevertheless the increasing need to be near supplies of coke and the declining reliance on water power, resulted in the industry beginning to move from its valley locations into the town where it became concentrated on the western and southern fringes. The urban setting did not result in any important organisational changes in the industry. The use of steam power allowed craftsmen to work uninterruptedly throughout the year, unworried by loss of volume of water in the summer months, but techniques did not change. The factory was largely foreign to the light steel trades and the small workshop continued to be the typical unit of manufacture. Here the independent workman ('the little mester') worked, sometimes for several large firms whose trade marks were stamped on the finished products. It was during this period of locational change in the industry that Thomas Boulsover invented Sheffield plate (steel coated with a thin coating of silver) which added another range of products to the cutlery and edge-tools for which the town was nationally and increasingly internationally renowned. By the beginning of the 1840s one-third of the workers in Sheffield parish (13,000 out of 39,000) were employed in the steel industry and of all the workers in the light steel trades in England and Wales, half lived in Sheffield.

The introduction and rapid growth of the railway network in the nineteenth century had a wide-reaching effect on Sheffield's steel industry. The railways opened up wider and larger markets, so that besides dominating the domestic trade in cutlery, Sheffield plate and edge tools, many Sheffield firms dominated the international market, especially in the Empire and the United States. From this period onwards every branch of the light trades became increasingly mechanised and medium-sized and large factories became general and premises still survive today on the western edge of the old town in the West Bar area and on the southern edge of the old town between Sheffield Moor and Pond Street (Figure 11.8).

Side by side with the expanding market for the light steel trades, was a completely new market for steel products: there was an insatiable demand from the 1850s for steel rails, machine parts, axles, tyres, boilers and springs for the railways, steel for guns and shells, and steel plates for ships. Throughout the 1850s before Bessemer's process allowed the large scale production of steel within a short time span, the

Figure 11.8. Empty Sheffield cutlery factory. The Author

coastal plants and those on easily mined orefields took advantage of their superior locations. Sheffield's steel industry then became a special steels industry, in which the research laboratory became as important as a good location in relation to pig iron or fuel supplies. Non-magnetic manganese steels for the electrical industries, chromium steels for shells, nickel steel for armour plate, stainless steels for rifle barrels and then for cutlery, all these and more were perfected in Sheffield. The introduction of basic openhearth steelmaking, electric arc melting and refining, automated rolling mills and other innovations all sustained the industry into the second half of the twentieth century.

It seemed that the Sheffield steel industry would go on for ever but the crash came at the end of the 1970s and early 1980s, the result of over-manning, over-capacity, insufficient capital

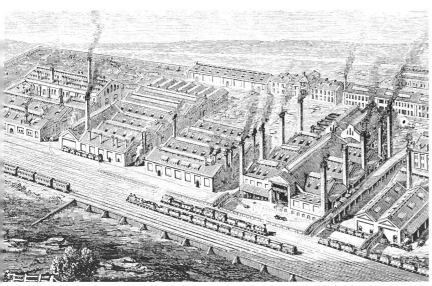

Figure 11.9. *Vickers, Sons and Company's River Don Works, Sheffield, in 1879. This was the greatest concentration of crucible steelmaking capacity in the world, capable of producing 15,000 tons of steel per annum.*

only way of producing large ingots was to assemble in one works a large number of crucibles and this led to the establishment of the first large steelworks in the wide, flat-floored lower Don valley to the east of the old town next to the river, the canal and the Sheffield to Rotherham railway (Figure 11.9). This development accelerated markedly after the introduction and adoption of Bessemer steel making after 1856, when five tons of steel could be made in half an hour in contrast to the two weeks it took to make a 50lb ingot of crucible steel (Figure 11.10).

In the 1860s and 1870s the concentration of Bessemer steel making in Sheffield made it the world's biggest producer of steel rails, but this was soon to change as

Figure 11.10. *Interior of the Bessemer Steelworks on Carlisle Street, Sheffield, 1879. The vertical converter on the left is 'blowing down a charge' while the steel from the horizontal one on the right is being tapped into a ladle. In the left foreground a workman is operating controls that tilted the converters and supplied the air blast that was an integral part of the Bessemer process of steelmaking. Bessemer's Sheffield steelworks was established to act as a model for other firms and to disseminate best practice.*

investment and strong overseas competition. Twenty thousand jobs in the steel industry were lost in Sheffield between 1979 and 1982 and the lower Don valley became a scene of devastation. Today, although the surviving firms produce more steel than at any time in the industry's history they do so in relatively few plants and with a much reduced workforce, and the continuously industrialised landscape in which they once operated stretching from the upper Don and its tributaries to Sheffield's lower Don valley and beyond to Parkgate and Kilnhurst has gone forever.

TEXTILES

South Yorkshire is not normally associated with the textile industry, but there was once a cotton mill on the Don in Sheffield, and those who visit the north-western parts of the county will have seen cottages with the traditional long wool weavers' windows on the upper floors, a reminder that the wool handloom weaving industry once extended southwards from West Yorkshire (Figure 11.11). What is even less well-known is that Barnsley was once one of the major centres of the linen weaving industry.

Linen manufacturing (weaving) was introduced to Barnsley in 1744 by Quakers from Cheshire and its steady growth ousted wire drawing from its position as the town's main manufacturing industry. Although the world's first steam-powered mill to manufacture linen yarn from flax was established in Leeds in 1792, the weaving of the yarn into linen fabrics was still mainly a domestic industry until the second half of the nineteenth century. The first power loom in Barnsley, for example, did not begin production until the 1830s and linen weaving on power looms in mills did not become the main means of production in the town until well into the 1860s. Until then most linen was made on handlooms (worked by manual labour) set up in a 'loomshop' in the cottage of a

Figure 11.11. Former wool handloom weaver's cottage, Thurlstone. The street on which the cottage stands is called Tenter Garth, the place where woollen cloth was stretched on frames and held in place by tenterhooks. Tom Randle

domestic weaver. The domestic weaver fetched yarn from the warehouse of a 'manufacturer' and wove his piece on a piecework basis to the directions of the manufacturer, before delivering the finished article, receiving payment, and collecting a further consignment of yarn. The manufacturers were usually owners of the cottages and looms.

Despite trading setbacks during the Napoleonic Wars and in the subsequent three decades up to 1847 during which the Corn Laws discouraged other trading nations from importing British goods, Barnsley became one of the greatest centres of linen production. At the time of the 1851 census Barnsley contained the greatest concentration of domestic linen weaving in Yorkshire, with over 4,000 handlooms located in the town in nearly 800 loomshops. Although domestic linen loomshops were widely distributed throughout the town, the greatest concentration lay between the bottom end of New Street in the north, Wood Street in the south, Silver Street in the west and Duke Street in the east, that is, the area known as the 'Barebones', with extensions eastwards along Copper Street and Union Street to Sheffield Road and beyond in Taylor Row, King Street and Rodney Row (Figure 11.12).

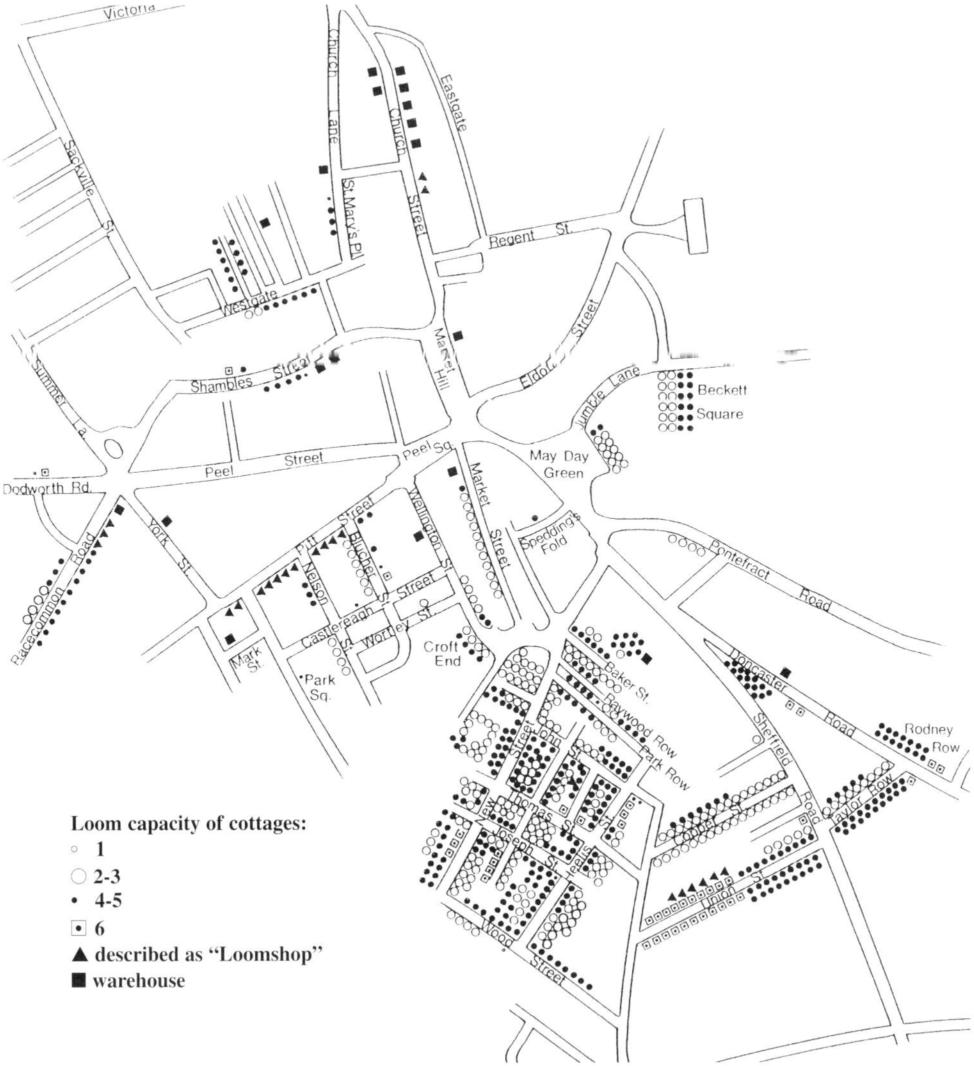

The looms were often located in cellars (a damp atmosphere meant less breaking of yarn) about six feet high, but not all cottages had cellars in which case looms could be located on the ground or upper floors. In order to admit light into the cellar loom shops, their ceilings were above ground level, allowing a window to be inserted to let in light and some air (the windows were generally closed, but with one pane missing). Because of the raised cellar roof, weavers' cottages had a characteristic short flight of steps leading up to the front door. Figure 11.13 shows a typical Barnsley weaver's cottage and cellar loomshop.

The linen weaving industry in Barnsley and in the country as a whole steadily but remorselessly became a factory industry in the second half of the nineteenth century, with spinning mills, weaving mills, bleachworks and calender works (where the cloth was rolled, smoothed and glazed).

Outside Barnsley the greatest changes were taking place in Belfast in Ulster.

Loom capacity of cottages:
- 1
- 2-3
- 4-5
- 6
- ▲ described as "Loomshop"
- ■ warehouse

Figure 11.12. Number and distribution of linen handloom weavers' cottages in Barnsley in 1848. Courtesy of Harold Taylor

Figure 11.13. A typical linen handloom weaver's cottage in Barnsley. The steps to the front door were typical and the result of raising the ceiling of the weaving shop in the cellar above street level to ensure light and ventilation.

Throughout the first half of the nineteenth century Belfast was steadily outstripping its domestic rivals in linen production but the weaving was still predominantly a domestic industry. In 1852 there was only one power loom in Belfast. Ten years later there were 6,000 and expansion continued throughout the nineteenth century.

Nearer to Barnsley, Leeds (including Hunslet) was also outstripping Barnsley. In 1851 the numbers employed in linen manufacture were about the same in the two towns (Barnsley, 3,729, Leeds-Hunslet, 3,927), but by 1861 only 2,538 persons were employed in linen manufacturing in Barnsley (a decline of 32 per cent in ten years) compared to 4,140 in Leeds-Hunslet (an increase of five per cent in ten years).

While the factory-based linen weaving industry was rapidly expanding in Belfast and was holding its own in Leeds-Hunslet, the industry in Barnsley failed to respond to new requirements and began a long and steady decline. Although Rowland Jackson in his *History of Barnsley* could report that in 1858 there were 4,000 handlooms and 1,000 power looms in the town, the industry was slow to adapt and as late as 1871 there were still about 1,200 handloom weavers in the town working outside the town's powerloom mills. Labour disputes throughout the second half of the nineteenth century deterred new investment in the industry and by 1875 there were only eight firms left in the town. This had decreased to four by 1908 and at the end of the First World War only two remained. The last mill closed in 1957.

Almost all of the evidence of linen manufacturing in the Barnsley area has disappeared. The handloom weavers' cottages have been swept away by slum clearance schemes, and the weaving mills which were once such major features of the townscape have long been demolished. All that remains are a manufacturer's warehouse in Westgate, a small number of bleachworks ponds and the more substantial remains of Cudworth bleachworks.

Places to visit

Interesting water power sites can be investigated at **Worsbrough Corn Mill** on the River Dove in Barnsley and at **Shepherd Wheel,** a cutler's wheel on the River Porter in Endcliffe Park in Sheffield. The earliest record of a water powered industrial site at Shepherd Wheel was in 1566. Two workshops are preserved, the dam is kept full and the iron overshot wheel is operated from time to time. **Abbeydale Industrial Hamlet,** on Abbeydale Road South, Sheffield, was a scythe making works for nearly two centuries and its dam, three water wheels, tilt-forge, crucible steel shop, grinding shop, warehouses and cottages have been preserved.

The best place to capture the atmosphere of a working wood where charcoal and whitecoal were made is in **Ecclesall Woods** in Sheffield. The woods contain many charcoal platforms and whitecoal pits and there is a monument to a charcoalmaker who was burnt to death in 1786. There are also areas in the woods where coppicing has been reinstated. Sheffield City Council's Countryside Management Unit has produced a leaflet about the woods: *Ecclesall Woods, Ancient Woodland.* A visit to Ecclesall Woods can be combined with one to the neighbouring Abbeydale Industrial Hamlet.

Caphouse Colliery in West Yorkshire (on the A42 between Wakefield and Huddersfield) is the centrepiece of the Yorkshire Mining Museum. There are permanent exhibitions about mining and visits can be made underground down the 450 feet deep shaft. At **Elsecar, the Heritage Centre** has an exhibition about the mining and ironmaking community, there is a Newcomen steam engine which was used to drain the collieries, and the fabric of the community, with its late eighteenth and early nineteenth century housing, survives.

The Top Forge, Wortley, once part of Wortley Ironworks is an industrial museum and includes a dam, sluices and waterwheels, and two water-powered tilt hammers with hand-operated cranes.

Kelham Island Museum, Alma Street, Sheffield, celebrates the life and work of industrial Sheffield and houses the River Don steam engine, and little mesters' workshops. At the entrance stands a Bessemer Converter.

What to read about the impact of industry on the South Yorkshire landscape

BARRACLOUGH, K. C. (1976) *Sheffield Steel,* Moorland Publishing Company.

CROSSLEY, D. (ed) (1989) *Water Power on the Sheffield Rivers,* Sheffield Trades Historical Society/ University of Sheffield.

COATES, B. and LEWIS, G.M. (1969) *The Doncaster Area: British Landscapes Through Maps 8,* Geographical Association.

DALTON, S., (1999) *Crashing Steel,* Wharncliffe Publishing.

ELLIOTT, B. (1988) ' Lime, liquor and leathermen: oak-bark tanning - the forgotten rural industry of South Yorkshire'. *Hallamshire Historian,* 2:1, 12-25.

FLEMING, A. (1995) 'Coal in the valley: mining in the Dearne valley at Wath' in M. Jones (ed) *Aspects of Rotherham 1,* Wharncliffe Publishing, pp. 220-240.

HAGUE, G. (1998) 'Colliery tramroads of north-west Rotherham' in M. Jones (ed) *Aspects of Rotherham 3,* Wharncliffe Publishing, pp. 153-169.

HEY, D., OLIVE, M., and LIDDAMENT, M (1997) *Forging the Valley,* Sheffield Academic Press.

JONES, M (1993) *Sheffield's Woodland Heritage,* (revised 2nd Edition), Green Tree Publications.

JONES, M. (1995) *Rotherham's Woodland Heritage,* Rotherwood Press.

JONES, M. (1995) 'Ironstone mining at Tankersley in the nineteenth century for Elsecar and Milton Ironworks' in B. Elliott (ed) *Aspects of Barnsley 3,* Wharncliffe Publishing, pp. 80-115.

LODGE, T. J. (1988) 'Rails from Stocksbridge'. *Hallamshire Historian,* 2:1, 25-30.

LODGE, T. (1997) 'The wrought iron era with recollections of Sheffield's last puddler' in M. Jones (ed) *Aspects of Sheffield 1,* Wharncliffe Publishing, pp. 153-166.

LODGE, T (1995) 'Rotherham's railway trades: an early chapter in heavy engineering' in M. Jones (ed) *Aspects of Rotherham 1,* Wharncliffe Publishing, pp. 241-272.

LODGE, T. (1999), 'Henry Bessemer, Sheffield's radical steelmaker' in M. Jones (ed) *Aspects of Sheffield 2,* Wharncliffe Publishing, pp. 164-181.

MACHAN, P. (1999) 'John Watts, Lambert Street: A surviving Sheffield firm with over 200 years' history' in M. Jones (ed) *Aspects of Sheffield 2,* Wharncliffe Publishing, pp. 79-96.

MEDLICOTT, I. (1998) ' Coal mining on the Wentworth estate, 1740-1840' in M. Jones (ed) *Aspects of Rotherham 3,* Wharncliffe Publishing, pp. 134-152.

MORLEY, C. (1997) 'A forgotten industry: the stove grate and light castings industry of Sheffield' in M. Jones (ed) *Aspects of Sheffield 1,* Wharncliffe Publishing, pp. 102-131.

MORLEY, C. (1998) 'The stove grate, range and decorative cast iron industry of Rotherham' in M. Jones (ed) *Aspects of Rotherham 3,* Wharncliffe Publishing, pp. 189-208.

ROGERS, A. (1995) 'Early watermills of the Maltby area' in M. Jones (Ed) *Aspects of Rotherham 1,* Wharncliffe Publishing, pp. 47-76.

TAYLOR, H. (1995) 'Taylor Row and the handloom weavers of Barnsley' in B. Elliott (ed) *Aspects of Barnsley 3,* Wharncliffe Publishing.

TWEEDALE, G. (1996) *The Sheffield Knife Book,* Hallamshire Press.

UMPLEBY, T. (1995) 'Water-power sites in the Dearne catchment: two Barnsley area corn mill examples' in B. Elliott (ed) *Aspects of Barnsley 3,* Wharncliffe Publishing, pp. 246-257.

TOWNSCAPES AND CITYSCAPES

SOUTH YORKSHIRE CONTAINS three very different types of town and city. There are the four large centres of Sheffield, Barnsley, Rotherham and Doncaster, all much enlarged and changed in the last two centuries. There is then another group of much smaller towns with long urban pedigrees but which did not share in the rapid expansion of the four largest centres; in this group are Tickhill, Bawtry, Penistone and Thorne. Lastly there are those places which developed urban characteristics relatively recently, largely as a result of the rapid expansion of coal mining and iron and steel making after 1850. In this category come places such as Wombwell, Wath, Mexborough, Maltby, Parkgate-Rawmarsh and Stocksbridge.

Limited space precludes a consideration in detail of all the places listed above. Instead detailed discussion is limited to Sheffield, by far the largest centre, Rotherham, as a representative of the second tier of town development, and Tickhill, Bawtry and Penistone, arguably the most attractive of the small towns in South Yorkshire.

SHEFFIELD

Sheffield is not only the largest of the urban centres in South Yorkshire, it has the most complicated structure and townscape. The pre-Domesday settlement grew up at the confluence of the Sheaf with the Don between the present Castlegate and Commercial Street. In the twelfth century a castle was built on the site now occupied by the Castle Market (see Chapter 7) and a church was erected on the site of the present cathedral. There was a market place under the castle walls. Between the fifteenth and seventeenth centuries Sheffield gained a

reputation for its edge tools and cutlery, but most of the workshops were along the Don, and its tributaries, the Sheaf, Porter, Rivelin and Loxley. One mill in the Loxley valley continued to use water power until 1959. These old water-powered sites are now important features of Sheffield's townscape as boating lakes, fishing ponds and wildlife refuges. In the late eighteenth century the steam engine was introduced and this led to the migration of a substantial proportion of Sheffield's staple trades into the town near coal

Figure 12.1. Sheffield in 1736 as depicted on Ralph Gosling's map. The axis of the medieval town from Lady's Bridge to the castle site, the market place and parish church is still clear. Note the water-powered sites on the rivers Don and Sheaf. In the west the town has encroached on the former open fields as shown by the curving streets between narrow building plots. Alsop Fields to the south were built over later in the century.

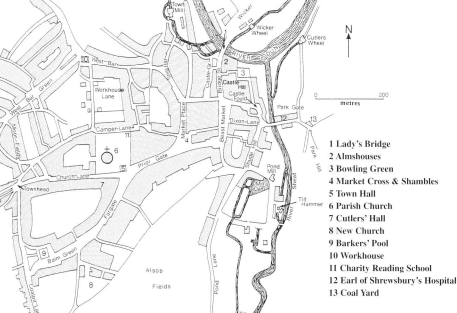

1 Lady's Bridge
2 Almshouses
3 Bowling Green
4 Market Cross & Shambles
5 Town Hall
6 Parish Church
7 Cutlers' Hall
8 New Church
9 Barkers' Pool
10 Workhouse
11 Charity Reading School
12 Earl of Shrewsbury's Hospital
13 Coal Yard

supplies though water-powered riverside workshops continued to be important. The new workshops were at first located around the western edges of the town but later colonised the former Alsop Fields area on the valley slopes above the Sheaf to the south of the old core. This area was laid out on a grid iron plan by the Duke of Norfolk between 1771 and 1778 as the street names testify: Howard Street (the family name), Surrey Street, Arundel Street (both minor titles), Earl Street, Charles Street (the Duke's first name), and Eyre Lane (the Duke's Sheffield agent's name). Mid-eighteenth century Sheffield, emerging from its medieval core, is shown in Figure 12.1.

The next phase of development was triggered by the commencement of the railway age. The canal did not reach its terminus in Wharf Street until 1819 (from 1751 its terminus had been at Tinsley) and only nineteen years later in 1838 the Sheffield to Rotherham Railway was opened giving Sheffield access to the York-London line. This was followed by the opening of a line to Manchester in 1845, to the Lincolnshire coast in 1849 and directly to London in 1870. The effect of these developments was to boost production in the edge-tool and cutlery trades resulting in the expansion of the town

(A)

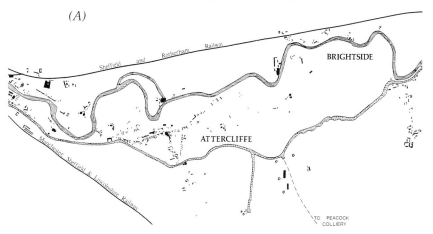

(B)

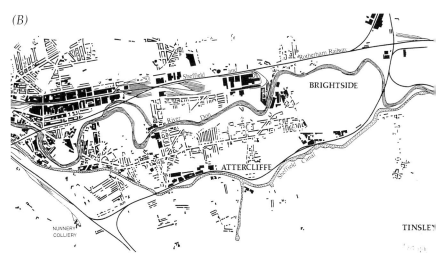

Figure 12.2. Transformation of the Lower Don valley between the early 1850s (A) and the early 1890s (B). Below: Sheffield from Attercliffe in 1830.

southwards and westwards towards Heeley and Crookes, and to create a completely new industry: the manufacture of heavy steel parts for the railway industry. The new industry required flat land and good transport facilities and this resulted in industrial ribbon development north-eastwards along the wide and flat Lower Don valley in Attercliffe, Brightside, Carbrook and Darnall, the works being surrounded by tightly packed terrace housing which eventually colonised the surrounding valley sides at Pitsmoor, Grimesthorpe and Wincobank. Figure 12.2 shows the transformation of the Lower Don valley between the 1850s and 1890s. By the latter date the production of common grade steel had been superseded by special steels and engineering.

The last quarter of the nineteenth century saw the steady growth of the city outwards, the result not only of the continued expansion of the light and heavy steel trades but also from the depopulation of the old core as streets were widened and houses and workshops gave way to offices and shops and places of entertainment to form a recognisable commercial central area. To the west and south-west new middle class suburbs developed, first in Broomhall and Nether Edge and then further out at Endcliffe, Ranmoor and Broomhill, the latter described by John Betjeman as 'the prettiest suburb in England' with its 'tree-shaded roads' and 'handsome mansions'.

Five major developments have changed and shaped Sheffield's cityscape in the twentieth century:
• slum clearance and redevelopment in the inner city (Figure 12.3) which has given Sheffield its high rise developments including tower blocks at Upperthorpe, Norfolk Park and Low Edges and the internationally 'known streets' in the sky at Park Hill, Hyde Park and Kelvin (now demolished);
• the continued outward residential growth of suburbs of

Figure 12.3. Post-war redevelopment in Sheffield; clearance of slums in Netherthorpe in the Middle Don Valley and their replacement by tower blocks.

owner-occupied housing in Crosspool, Fulwood, Ecclesall and Beauchief in the south-west and south, and of municipal housing estates in the east and north at places such as the Manor, Woodthorpe, Arbourthorne, Intake and Gleadless Valley, Firth Park, Longley and Parson Cross;
• the absorption and suburbanisation of former West Riding communities at Stannington, Loxley, Worrall, Oughtibridge, Ecclesfield, Grenoside, Chapeltown and High Green and of the former Derbyshire villages of Mosbrough, Norton, Dore and Totley;
• the decline of the heavy steel and engineering industry in the Lower Don Valley (employment declined from 40,000 to 13,000 between 1975 and 1988) and the emergence there of a new mix of land uses dominated not by industry but entertainment and

Figure 12.4. Meadowhall in the Lower Don valley in the 1990s, looking south-west. Dominating the site once occupied by Hadfield's Steel Works is the Meadowhall Shopping Centre with 1.2 million square feet of shopping space and parking for 11,000 cars. The River Don almost encircles the shopping centre in a large meander. Across a bridge on the right (north-west) is the terminus of the Lower Don Valley arm of the supertram system, main line railway stations and bus interchange. In the foreground is the M1 motorway. Meadowhall Leisure Shopping

shopping, aided by the presence of the M1 motorway and the development of the supertram network (see Figure 12.4);
• schemes to maintain and enhance the attractiveness of the central area such as inner ring roads, pedestrianisation and most recently developments on the city campus site of Sheffield Hallam University, and the ongoing developments around the Town Hall complex including the re-design of the Peace Gardens.

ROTHERHAM

Rotherham's origins, like those of Sheffield, lie beside an important river crossing, this time of the River Don below its confluence with the Rother. The bridge still has one of only three surviving bridge chapels in the country (Figure 12.5). The chapel, built of 'Rotherham Red' sandstone, was constructed in the late fifteenth century and travellers could give thanks for their safe arrival in the town or pray for a safe journey when leaving it. The old town grew up on the eastern bank of the river where a low bluff provided a commanding site for the parish church, rebuilt at the end of the middle ages in the Perpendicular style, and which has dominated the town ever since (Figure 12.5). It is generally regarded as one of the most magnificent parish churches in Yorkshire. Before industrialisation Rotherham was a prosperous market town with its market place occupying a site south-west of the church. The compact medieval town grew up around the churchyard and market place with extensions along Bridgegate, Westgate, Moorgate, Wellgate and Doncaster Gate.

The second half of the nineteenth century saw the northward extension of the old town on land owned by the Earl of Effingham (whose name is enshrined in the street names Effingham, Howard and Frederick) and on the Eastwood estate. Industrial development had come earlier, the greatest stimulus coming from the Walker Brothers' foundry

Figure 12.5. *The skyline of Rotherham has been dominated by its late fifteenth century parish church, described by Sir Nicholas Pevsner as 'one of the largest and stateliest of parish churches in Yorkshire.' In the foreground stands the chapel bridge with its late medieval chapel.*

established in 1745-46 to the east of the Don in Masbrough which was rapidly to become Rotherham's industrial satellite before becoming an integral part of the town. The ironfounding tradition established by the Walkers gave birth to Rotherham's important railway engineering industry, its stove grate industry and eventually its steel industry dominated by Steel, Peech and Tozer's Templeborough Steelworks. In its heyday heavy industry dominated the flat land beside the Don from Tinsley in the south to Parkgate in the north.

Industrial development and an expansion of the town's professional class gave rise to one of the most remarkable residential developments in South Yorkshire in the nineteenth century: the colonisation of Moorgate by Rotherham's most

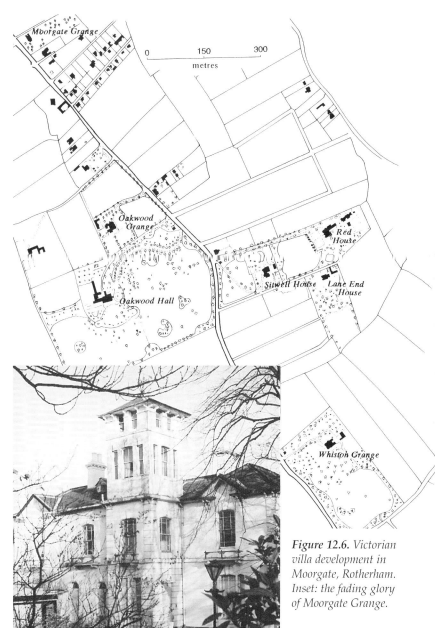

Figure 12.6. *Victorian villa development in Moorgate, Rotherham. Inset: the fading glory of Moorgate Grange.*

successful industrialists and professional men (Figure 12.6). Moorgate Grange was owned by John Guest (of Guest & Chrimes' foundry) before passing to the Chrimes family; Oakwood Hall in its extensive grounds was built for William Yates, stovegrate manufacturer and survives as part of the Rotherham general hospital; Oakwood Grange was built for Yates' daughter; Red House was the home of the Micklethwaits, another stovegrate manufacturing family; and Whiston Grange belonged to Frederick Parker Rhodes, solicitor, and Lane End House to his brother Charles, mining engineer.

Rotherham's twentieth century suburban development includes interesting early municipal housing. In the ten years between 1919 and 1929 Rotherham Corporation built more than 2,500 new houses mainly on the East Dene and Herringthorpe estates. In some of the earliest developments a variety of housing types was used, in great contrast to the monotony of later local authority building.

TICKHILL

Tickhill is the pleasantest small town in South Yorkshire. Despite the inevitable suburban expansion, the centre of the town still has the air of an ancient market town unaffected by industrialisation (Figure 12.7). This atmosphere is enhanced by the fact that the centre of the town has two rookeries, and the churchyard is carpeted by celandines in spring, giving it a very traditional atmosphere - what visitors from abroad expect a small English country town to be like. Yet Tickhill did not grow naturally from an ancient village into a market town - it was an artificial foundation, a planned medieval town established by a Norman lord to serve his estate and his main residence - and the visitor to the town can clearly see how everything evolved.

The town of Tickhill did not exist when the Domesday survey was carried out in 1086. The nearest place mentioned was Dadsley. It is not clear exactly where this settlement lay as no signs have been found on the ground or through aerial photography. It was probably sited near Dadsley Well and Dadsley Lane about half a mile north of the town. A church existed to serve Dadsley and neighbouring settlements and the site of this is at All Hallows Hill again to the north of the present town.

Tickhill, as has already been pointed out in Chapter 7, means Tica's Hill and it came into existence sometime between 1086 and 1100 when the Norman lord Roger de Busli decided to build his castle there. The castle was dominated by the motte, 75 feet high and 80 feet in diameter on which a timber and then an eleven-sided stone keep (1178-82) was built. Below the motte was an elevated **inner bailey** covering two acres bounded by a curtain wall and then surrounded by a water filled moat. Although the motte and inner bailey are now private land, the visitor to Tickhill can walk round the western and southern boundaries and see the water filled moat, the remains of the curtain wall and gatehouse to the inner bailey,

Figure 12.7. Tickhill, looking north from the castle towards the parish church which stood within a protected outer bailey. The Author

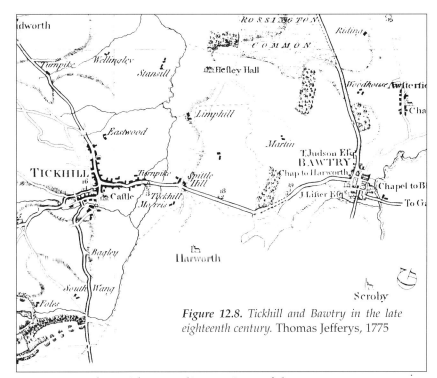

Figure 12.8. Tickhill and Bawtry in the late eighteenth century. Thomas Jefferys, 1775

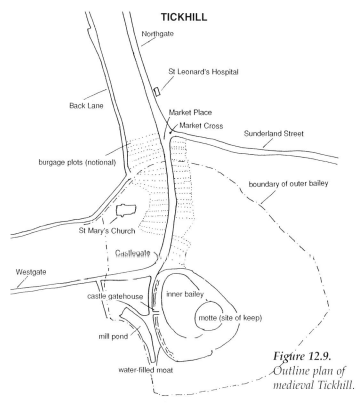

Figure 12.9. Outline plan of medieval Tickhill.

together with more distant views of the motte.

Encircling the inner bailey, and extending some distance to the east and north was probably another defended space, the outer boundary of which was marked by a ditch whose location was identified during an excavation in 1975. This was the outer bailey. To the west this area contained a mill pond (still in existence). To the north the **outer bailey** extended as far north as the market place and included the parish church and churchyard within its boundaries.

The new town built under the protection of the castle was basically a one street town (see Figures 12.8 and 12.9), extending northwards from the eastern end of Westgate, up

Castlegate to Northgate (-gate (*gata*) is Old Norse for street). The earliest town was probably restricted to Castlegate with the market place at its northern end. Running off the central part of the market place eastwards is Sunderland Street. Sunderland means land 'put asunder' for a special purpose, possibly a market and fairground - Tickhill has had a weekly market and annual fair from its foundation. Eventually the medieval town expanded westwards along Westgate, northwards along Northgate and eastwards along Sunderland Street. Only in the second half of the twentieth century has the old medieval town been surrounded by the usual outbreak of what one local writer earlier this century called 'scarlatina' - red brick suburbs that could be anywhere.

A feature of the original medieval town is that property boundaries ran back from Castlegate and Northgate in the form of long narrow burgage plots, enabling the maximum number of tradesmen and craftsmen to have a street frontage to serve tenants coming to pay their rents, travellers moving north or south and the rural population from the surrounding area every market day. Significantly in Tickhill, old maps show the burgage plots to be narrowest near the market place, where competition for a street frontage would have been most severe. An example of a long burgage plot can be seen in Tickhill by entering the coaching yard of the *Red Lion* Inn which has been turned into a specialised shopping area called St Mary's Court.

The outstanding building in Tickhill is St Mary's parish church. Originally built in the thirteenth century to replace All Hallows at Dadsley, it was enlarged in the fourteenth and fifteenth centuries and is one of the outstanding Perpendicular churches in South Yorkshire. It is built from Magnesian Limestone and both inside and out can only be described as stately. It has a wonderful tower, 124 feet high with four figures in niches on its four faces and the church contains magnificent stone tombs, stone coffins, iron-bound wooden chests, medieval stained glass and early Victorian pews with cast iron poppy heads.

BAWTRY

Bawtry rivals Tickhill in its attractiveness, and the reason is the same: it was by-passed by modern industrialisation and central redevelopment. It shares with Tickhill a planned medieval origin that is evident in the modern townscape.

Although now in South Yorkshire, the site of Bawtry was originally in the northern corner of the Nottinghamshire ecclesiastical parish of Blyth. The planned town was laid out towards the end of the twelfth century by the manorial lord to reap the benefits of the river trade that was conducted from the banks of the River Idle at the junction of the Great North Road with the land route westwards (the modern A631) to the towns of Rotherham and Sheffield (Figure 12.8). To the west lay a landlocked hinterland stretching for more than 40 kilometres to the Pennines; to the east lay access to the Trent (at West Stockwith, just 10 kilometres away, where seagoing ships could dock) and the Humber, and beyond that to the east coast of England and the continent. Within two decades the new town had the right of a fair (1213/14), and by 1247 a market was in existence. Its prosperity waxed and waned over the centuries in tune with the national and regional economy. John Leland who visited the town about 1540 said it was a 'very bare and poore market-town'. More fulsome was Daniel Defoe who described Bawtry's river port trade in the 1720s thus:

...they bring down ...lead, from the lead mines and smelting-houses of Derbyshire, wrought iron and edge-tools, of all sorts, from the forges at Sheffield, and from the country call'd Hallamshire, being adjacent to the towns of Sheffield and Rotherham ... Also millstones and grindstones, in very great quantities are brought down and shipped off here, and so carry'd by sea to Hull and to London, and even to Holland also.

The river trade was to decline with improvements to the River Don which gradually pushed the head of navigation westwards, reaching Tinsley basin in 1751. This was followed by the completion of the Chesterfield Canal in 1777 allowing north Derbyshire goods to go directly to West Stockwith. But Bawtry's location on the Great North Road meant that it could take full advantage of the increased traffic of the turnpike era, and it gradually turned its back on the river. The Great North Road became its focus, and it became a leading coaching town until the coming of the railways. After another period of stagnation of nearly a century, from the 1920s until 1960 the town once again became a major stopping place for travellers by car, when the construction of the A1(M) meant that the town was by-passed by through traffic.

Bawtry's planned medieval origins are evident in the vestiges which remain of its grid-iron plan in streets such as the roughly north-south High Street and Top Lane, and the roughly east-west Scot Lane, Wharf Street, Church Walk, and Swan Street. St Nicholas' parish church (St Nicholas is the patron saint of seafarers) is on the eastern edge of the planned town near the former wharf on the Idle suggesting that the port pre-dates the planned town. The meander in the river on whose banks the port lay, was straightened when the railway entered the town at that point, but the county boundary still follows the line of the meander. Few vestiges of the river port and its merchant inhabitants have survived but notable exceptions are the late seventeenth century Dutch House at the corner of Church Street and Wharf Street with its swirling Dutch gables suggesting trading links by its owner with the Low Countries, the Ship Inn at the southern end of Church Street, on the site of a much earlier inn, and the former merchant's house in the Market Place which is now Barton's garage.

It was the prosperous years of the coaching era of the second half of the eighteenth century and the first half of the nineteenth century that gave Bawtry much of its present character, especially along High Street, around the Market Place and on South Parade. Here the coaching inn, *The Crown*, handsome Georgian houses, and elegant terraces have survived.

PENISTONE

Penistone's role as a market town was secured in 1699 when Godfrey Bosville of Gunthwaite, local landowner and magistrate, obtained for it a market charter which superseded a grant of a Tuesday market and three-day fair to Elias de Midhope, manorial lord of Langsett, at an unidentified place called Penisale. Tradition has it that this market and fair were held three kilometres south-west of Penistone around an ancient yew tree near Alderman's Head overlooking Langsett village.

Penistone's claim for a market was largely based on the difficulty of getting to other nearby markets at Barnsley and Huddersfield because of the state of the roads in winter (animals as well as farmers and their families had to walk to and from the market).

For more than 200 years of its existence Penistone did not have a dedicated market place, the market being held principally in St Mary's Street and Market St (Figure 12.10), with temporary hurdle enclosures penning sheep. Penistone eventually gained a reputation for the quality of its dairy cows, with buyers coming from Manchester and Salford by the nineteenth century. It was not until 1910 that a formally

Figure 12.10. Penistone market day, early twentieth century. Before the construction of the purpose-built Cattle Market in 1910, Penistone's beast market was held in the main streets of the town. Cattle, sheep, pigs, and in this case farm horses, vied with people for right of way on market days. The horses are on Market Street with St Mary's Street in the background. The parish church is just out of shot on the right. Chris Sharpe, Old Barnsley

planned market place was opened. Penistone also boasted a cloth hall, but its domestic weaving industry (linen and wool) eventually withered away and the cloth hall was converted to other uses.

In plan, the old core of Penistone is long and narrow, causing the writer of the description of Penistone in White's Directory in 1838 to state that it consisted 'principally of one wide street, in which there are a few neat houses'. The old town extends from the Barnsley Road in the north up Bridge Street and St Mary's Street to the western end of Church Street and Shrewsbury Road where the medieval parish church and modern market place are located at the highest point in the old town, and then along Market Street which gives way to modern suburbs, which also surround the old town on east and west. The railway which first came to Penistone in 1845 not only gave Penistone its most outstanding architectural feature - the 29-arch Penistone viaduct (1849) - but also industry, principally Cammell Laird's Bessemer Steel Works (1864-1930), spawning an industrial district on the eastern side of the town beside the River Don and the railway. A 'model village' - Cubley - constructed of concrete made to simulate stone blocks - was erected in 1921-22 to accommodate the Cammell Laird workers, the unlikely architect being Sir Herbert Baker, who had worked on New Delhi with Sir Edward Lutyens.

What to read about South Yorkshire's townscapes and cityscapes

BEASTALL, T. (1997) *Tickhill: Portrait of a Country Town*, The Waterdale Press.
BROWNHILL, R. N. (1987) *The Penistone Scene*, Bridge Publications.
CROSSLAND, PHYLLIS (1995) 'Penistone Market' in B. Elliott (Ed) *Aspects of Barnsley 3*, Wharncliffe Publishing, pp. 230-240.
FINE, D. (1992) Sheffield: History and Guide, Alan Sutton.

HEY, D, OLIVE, M., and LIDDAMENT, M. (1997) *Forging the Valley*, Sheffield Academic Press.
HEY, D. (1998) *A History of Sheffield*, Carnegie Publishing.
HOLLAND, D. (1999) 'Bawtry: History in the Landscape' in B. Elliott (Ed) *Aspects of Doncaster 2*, Wharncliffe Publishing, pp. 169-174.
MUNFORD, A. P. (1994) *Rotherham: A Pictorial History*, Phillimore.
MUNFORD, T. (1995) 'From Slums to Council Houses' in M. Jones (Ed) *Aspects of Rotherham 1*, Wharncliffe Publishing, pp. 273 to 297.

Places to visit

There are several publications that are useful accompaniments to a walk around **Sheffield.** David Fine's *Sheffield: History and Guide* contains three walking tours (The Centre, The Porter and The Lower Don). The Hallamshire Press has published three East End history trails: 1. *The Sheffield and Tinsley Canal*, 2. *The Attercliffe History Trail* and 3. *The Five Weirs Walk*. Melvyn Jones's *The Porter Valley* (Sheffield Countryside Management Unit) takes the user on a guided walk from Hunter's Bar to Fulwood Head with spectacular views back over the city.

The old town in **Rotherham** can be explored with the aid of *A Walk Around Rotherham: The Town Centre* (Rotherham Central Library, Archives and Local Studies Section, 1994) or the *Town Centre Trail* (Rotherham Library Service, no date). For those particularly interested in the varied use of building materials, *The Building Stones of Rotherham* by Michael Clark can be thoroughly recommended (Clifton Park Museum, 1995).

Tickhill, Bawtry and **Penistone** are all worth a half day trip. Go on a weekday to get a feel of a small market town going about its business (market day in Penistone is on Thursdays). Do not forget to visit the parish church in each case.